101 POWERFUL
MAGIC SPELLS
FOR BABY WITCHES

Easy To Follow, Powerful and Real Spells

for Budding Beginner Witches

BY HAZEL EVERMORE

The Lost Book Project

© 2023, The Lost Book Project. All rights reserved.

Published by The Lost Book Project
124 City Road
London, EC1V 2NX. United Kingdom
www.TheLostBookProject.com

ISBN: 978-1-7384637-0-1

Library of Congress Cataloging-in-Publication Data

Names: Evermore, Hazel, author.
Title: 101 Powerful Spells for Baby Witches / Hazel Evermore.
Description: London: The Lost Book Project, 2023
Identifiers: ISBN 978-1-7384637-0-1
Subjects: LCSH Witchcraft. | Magic. | Wicca.
Classification: LCC BF1566 .E96 2023 | DDC 133.4/3—dc23

Cover Design: Luisa

The information in this book is intended to be educational and not for diagnosis, prescription, or treatment of any health disorder whatsoever. This book is not a substitute for medical advice, and the author and publisher expressly disclaim responsibility for any adverse effects arising from the use or application of the information contained herein.

Printed in United Kingdom

First Edition

TABLE OF CONTENTS

FOREWORD

It is with great pleasure and a deep sense of honor that I, Hazel Evermore, present to you "101 Powerful Spells for Baby Witches." This book is more than just a collection of spells; it is a gateway to a journey that is as ancient as time yet as new as each breath we take. It is a journey into the heart of witchcraft, a path that I have walked for over two decades with reverence, wonder, and an ever-growing sense of discovery.

Witchcraft, in its essence, is an intimate dance with the natural world, a dialogue with the unseen forces that animate our universe. It is a practice rooted in empowerment, wisdom, and the transformative power of intention. This book is born out of my own journey in the craft, out of the countless lessons learned and the insights gained along the way. It is written with the hope that it will light a spark in you, the reader, to explore the boundless possibilities of your own magical potential.

As you turn these pages, you will find spells that have been crafted with care and intention, designed to be accessible to beginners yet rich in symbolism and meaning. These spells are more than just words and rituals; they are invitations to connect deeply with the elements, to tune into your inner wisdom, and to harness the power that resides within and all around you.

But "101 Powerful Spells for Baby Witches" is not just about learning to cast spells. It is about embarking on a journey of self-discovery and personal empowerment. Witchcraft is a path that encourages you to look within, to question, to explore, and to grow. It is a path that challenges you to confront your shadows, embrace your light, and find your unique place in the tapestry of life.

As you embark on this journey, remember that witchcraft is as individual as the practitioner. There is no single "right" way to walk this path; there is only your way. So, I encourage you to use this book not as a rigid manual, but as a guide, a source of inspiration, and a starting point for your own exploration and experimentation.

In closing, I extend my heartfelt wishes to you for a journey filled with discovery, empowerment, and magic. May the spells in this book be your companions and guides as you step into the wondrous world of witchcraft. May they inspire you to uncover the magic that lies within you and all around you.

Welcome to your magical journey.

Blessed be,

Hazel Evermore

CHAPTER 1.
INTRODUCTION

Welcome to "101 Magic Spells for Baby Witches," your enchanting guidebook into the whimsical world of witchcraft. Whether you stumbled upon this tome out of curiosity, a deep-seated knowing, or a serendipitous whisper from the universe, you are exactly where you're meant to be.

In these pages lies a trove of spells—each a thread in the tapestry of magic that you're about to weave. As a baby witch, you stand on the precipice of discovery, where every incantation is a step, every potion a journey, and every charm a dance with the divine. This book is more than just a collection of spells; it's a gateway to a new perspective, a re-enchantment of the mundane, and a means to empower your innermost self.

You'll find that these spells are crafted with simplicity in mind, for magic is not about complexity but about intention. Your will, your desire, and your heart are the most potent ingredients you can bring to any magical working. So, fret not about having a cauldron or a wand—though they do have their charm. Instead, focus on honing your intuition and listening to the whispers of nature and the murmurs of your soul.

Here, we begin with the easiest of spells to warm your spirit and guide your hands. As you progress, the spells will grow with you, evolving and deepening as your magical prowess flourishes. From the gentle touch of a healing charm to the protective embrace of a home blessing, your journey will be as varied as it is vibrant.

Magic is not reserved for the chosen few; it is the birthright of everyone who dares to reach for it. In "101 Magic Spells for Baby Witches," you are the architect of your own destiny, the weaver of your dreams, and the custodian of an ancient wisdom that thrums through the ages.

As you turn these pages, do so with an open heart and a curious mind. Let joy be your compass and wonder your path. The world is brimming with magic, dear witchling, and it's time for you to claim your piece of the wonder.

With every spell you cast, remember: you are the magic. Welcome to your bewitching journey. Welcome home.

CHAPTER 2.
WHAT IS A SPELL?

If you've ever made a wish on a dandelion or whispered your hopes to the stars, you've touched the edge of what it means to cast a spell. A spell is a deliberate and conscious act intended to harness the energies of the world and your own will to bring about change. It is poetry in motion, a sacred dialogue between you and the universe.

A spell can be as simple as a spoken word, as intricate as a ceremonial rite, or as casual as scribbling symbols on a paper. It is a focused intention, a crafted desire made tangible through words, objects, and actions aligned with your goal. When you cast a spell, you are asking—no, telling— the universe that you are ready for transformation, that you are open to the shifting tides of magic to work in your favor.

But what truly is a spell? It's an embodiment of hope, a vessel for your dreams. It is the art of seeing what is not yet visible, of weaving potential into reality. A spell is your heart's deepest desire given wings. It's not just about changing the world around you; it's about changing yourself, growing in strength, wisdom, and power with every word you utter, every candle you light, every herb you crush.

In this book, we'll explore the essence of a spell. We'll delve into the components that make a spell work, the timing that aligns it with the cosmos, and the focus that propels it from your inner world into the outer one. You'll learn that every spell you cast is a step on the path of self-discovery, a step towards becoming the witch—and the person—you are meant to be.

So, dear witchling, let us begin by unraveling the mystery of spells. Let's understand their structure, their substance, and the spark of magic that lives within them. Let us journey together through the dance of casting spells, and in doing so, may we discover not just the power of the universe, but the power within ourselves.

History of Spellcasting

In the tapestry of human history, spellcasting is a thread that winds through every culture, civilization, and epoch. It is as ancient as the first whispered wishes of humanity and as varied as the many peoples of the Earth. To delve into the history of spellcasting is to embark on a journey through time and thought, exploring how our ancestors sought to influence their world through the unseen forces of magic.

The roots of spellcasting stretch back to the prehistoric times when shamans and wise women communed with the spirits of nature and invoked their powers for the benefit of their tribes. These early practitioners were seen as mediators between the physical world and the spiritual realm, and their spells were deeply interwoven with the rhythms of the earth and the cycles of the moon and sun.

As civilizations rose, so too did the sophistication of magical practices. The Egyptians, with their rich pantheon of gods and goddesses, crafted spells that were inscribed on papyrus and tomb walls, intended to protect the living and guide the dead in the afterlife. The use of amulets, potions, and incantations was commonplace, and the knowledge of such magics was both feared and revered.

In the ancient Greco-Roman world, spellcasting was a multifaceted practice. The Greeks had their oracles and mystery cults, where initiates were taught secret spells and rites. The Romans, too, had their vestal virgins and augurs, who performed public rituals to ensure the favor of the gods for the state, and private curses were etched on tablets to bring misfortune to enemies.

The Middle Ages brought a dichotomy in the perception of magic. On one hand, the wise folk of the villages continued the ancient practices of healing and protection, casting spells that were often a blend of pagan tradition and early Christian prayers. On the other hand, the rise of the Inquisition brought about a dark period where the practice of spellcasting was often equated with witchcraft and heresy, leading to persecution and tragedy.

The Renaissance revived interest in the esoteric aspects of spellcasting, with scholars rediscovering ancient texts and translating them into the vernacular. The printing press allowed for the wider dissemination of magical knowledge, and grimoires—manuals of magic that included instructions for casting spells—became increasingly popular.

In modern times, the practice of spellcasting has seen a renaissance of its own, with the rise of new age movements and a revival of pagan religions such as Wicca. Today, spellcasting is often viewed through a lens of personal spirituality and empowerment, a way for individuals to connect with the divine forces of the universe and manifest their desires.

Throughout its history, spellcasting has been a reflection of the hopes, fears, and desires of humanity. It has evolved with our societies, adapted to our changing beliefs, and yet remains, at its core, a primal expression of our need to influence the world around us. Whether through the smoke of a shaman's fire or the chant of a modern-day witch, the art of spellcasting continues to enchant and inspire, a testament to the enduring power of belief and the human spirit.

Spellcasting and Witchcraft Today

In today's world, spellcasting and witchcraft have emerged from the shadows of history into the light of modern understanding and acceptance. They represent not just a resurgence of old practices, but a new wave of personal empowerment and spiritual discovery.

Witchcraft today is as diverse as the practitioners who follow the path. It is no longer bound by the strict dogmas or the secretive covens of the past. Instead, it has blossomed into a global community where knowledge is shared freely, and practices are adapted to individual beliefs and cultural backgrounds. The internet has become a digital cauldron where witches of all levels of experience exchange spells, wisdom, and experiences.

Contemporary spellcasting is often seen as a form of self-care, a way to assert one's will over personal circumstances. It's as much about manifesting positive changes in one's life as it is about connecting with the natural world and the energies that flow through it. Spells are cast for love, healing, protection, and prosperity, reflecting the universal desires of the human heart.

In this age of environmental awareness, many witches are turning to eco-friendly and sustainable practices, honoring the Earth and seeking to balance the energies taken with those given back. The green witch works with the land, the kitchen witch with the hearth, and the urban witch finds magic in the heartbeat of the city. Each brings their unique perspective to the craft, enriching it with their experiences and insights.

The practice of witchcraft is also increasingly intersectional, acknowledging and embracing the diversity of those who walk its paths. It is a sanctuary for people of all genders, sexual orientations, ethnic backgrounds, and walks of life, each bringing their voice and their magic to the collective table.

Spellcasting in modern witchcraft is also characterized by a blending of traditions. It's not uncommon for a witch to draw upon the practices of multiple cultures, creating a personalized form of magic that resonates with their individual spirit. This eclectic approach allows for a rich and ever-evolving practice that honors the past while forging new traditions.

Despite its growth and evolution, the core of witchcraft remains the same: it is a celebration of the power within and around us. It is a dance with the divine, an acknowledgment of the web of life that connects all things. Today's witches continue to cast spells, not in the hopes of bending the will of the gods, but in the belief that they are co-creators with the universe, shaping their destinies through will, word, and the wisdom of the craft.

Spellcasting and witchcraft today stand as a testament to the enduring human need for connection, empowerment, and the magic that arises when we dare to dream. It is a vibrant, living tradition that continues to grow, adapt, and thrive in the modern world, offering sanctuary, strength, and a touch of enchantment to all who seek its wisdom.

CHAPTER 3.
HOW TO CAST
A SPELL?

As a new witch stepping into the realm of magic, the process of casting a spell may seem shrouded in mystery, but fear not, for it is a path well-trodden by many before you. This chapter is your guide to understanding the essence of spell casting, to demystify the process and give you an overview of how magic is woven.

At its heart, casting a spell is an act of focused intention. It's about aligning your deepest desires with the natural energies of the world. Imagine for a moment that the universe is a vast ocean, and your spell is a bottle carrying your message. With the right preparation and mindset, you can send your message out to sea, trusting the currents to carry it to its destination.

Now, how does one begin? The process is both simple and profound. First, it starts with clarity—knowing what you want to achieve. This clarity is the compass that guides your spell. Without a clear destination, your magical bottle might drift aimlessly. But with a precise intention, the path becomes apparent, and the universe can conspire to help you.

Next is the gathering of your tools and symbols—each chosen to represent and amplify aspects of your intention. Think of these as the ingredients in a recipe, each adding its unique flavor to the final dish. In spell casting, these could be crystals that resonate with love for a love spell or herbs known for their protective qualities for a protection spell.

Creating a sacred space is also crucial. It is a space where you feel at one with yourself and the universe—a place where the mundane does not distract from the magical. This can be anywhere that feels right to you, where you can meditate, focus, and be at peace.

Then comes the actual casting. This is where you bring together your tools, your intention, and your emotional energy. It is a ritual, a sacred dance where your movements, words, and thoughts weave together to form the spell. Your will is the thread that binds these elements, and your emotional energy is the knot that ties it all together.

Finally, trust is an essential ingredient. Once cast, you must trust in the natural order, in the ebb and flow of energies, to carry your spell to fruition. Doubt can cloud the waters and misdirect your bottle. Trust, coupled with patience, allows the spell to work in the time and manner that is best for you.

Remember, dear beginner, this is just an overview. You will now learn more about each of these steps in detail. You will learn to select your tools with intuition, create your sacred space with reverence, and cast your spells with confidence. Each spell you cast will be a stepping stone on your journey into the craft, and with each step, you will grow in knowledge, power, and connection to the magic that weaves through all things.

Defining Your Intention

In the realm of spellcasting, your intention is the seed from which the spell grows; it is the soul of your magical work. The clearer and more focused your intention, the more potent your spell will be. Intention is not just a wish or a hope; it is a determined direction of will. It is the force that propels the spell into the universe, shaping energy according to your purpose.

The first step in any spell is to define your intention with precision. This means taking the time to reflect on what you truly want to achieve. It's not enough to have a vague desire for 'happiness' or 'love.' Instead, drill down to the specifics. What kind of love are you seeking? What would happiness look like for you? The more specific you are, the more targeted your spell can be.

Your intention should also be phrased positively. Instead of focusing on what you don't want, focus on what you do. The universe responds to positive energy. For instance, if you wish to banish anxiety, frame your intention around finding peace or courage, rather than simply escaping the anxiety.

The Role of Intentions in Spells

The intention is the driving force behind the energy of your spell. It's what guides the energy to form the outcome you desire. When you cast a spell without a clear intention, the energy can become scattered and ineffective. It's like trying to hit a target in the dark. With a clear intention, you turn on the light, aim, and direct your energy to hit the bullseye.

Your intention also serves as an invitation to the universe to work on your behalf. It's you declaring, "This is what I want, and I am ready to receive it." This declaration opens the channels of energy and begins the process of manifestation.

How to Work with Intentions

Working with intentions begins with stillness. Find a quiet space to meditate on your desires. Write down what you want to accomplish with your spell. Use this written statement to refine and clarify your intention until it resonates deeply with you.

Once you have your intention, it should be woven into every part of your spell. If you're using candles, choose a color that corresponds with your intention. If you're using herbs, select those known for aiding in manifestations like yours. As you perform your spell, keep your intention at the forefront of your mind. Visualize it as a beacon, glowing with the energy of your will.

Remember, intentions are not just thoughts; they are commitments. When you cast a spell, you commit to the change you wish to see. This commitment must be carried not just in your spell but in your actions and thoughts afterward. By aligning your actions with your intention, you reaffirm the energy of the spell and maintain the momentum needed to manifest your desire.

In essence, understanding and defining your intention is the cornerstone of effective spellcasting. It shapes the energy, directs the flow, and determines the outcome. Treat it with the reverence it deserves, and you will find your spells imbued with a power that is as profound as it is personal.

Choosing Your Tools

The act of spellcasting is a sacred ritual, and the tools you choose serve as physical manifestations of your intentions, each adding a layer of depth and complexity to your spell. They are the vessels that will carry your wishes into the realms of the unseen. While not all spells require tools, incorporating them can enhance your focus and symbolize your commitment to the work at hand.

Candles: The Guiding Light

Candles are a staple in spellcasting due to their ability to symbolize the element of fire, which represents transformation, creation, and destruction. The flame of a candle is like a beacon, illuminating your intentions and sending them out into the universe. Each color holds different energies: green for growth and prosperity, red for passion and strength, blue for healing and peace, and so on. Select a candle color that aligns with your spell's purpose, and as it burns, envision your intention being released with the smoke and light.

Crystals: Earth's Concentrated Energies

Crystals and gemstones are the earth's way of offering us concentrated energies. Each type of crystal holds specific properties that can align with various intentions. Rose quartz promotes love and harmony, amethyst is known for its psychic and protective qualities, and citrine is believed to attract wealth and abundance. When choosing a crystal, hold it in your hand and see if its energy resonates with your intention. You can place crystals on your altar, carry them with you, or even incorporate them into jewelry to keep their energies close.

Herbs: The Fragrance of Magic

Herbs have been used in magic for millennia, each with its own signature properties. Lavender can be used for purification and calmness, sage for cleansing and wisdom, and basil for wealth and success. Herbs can be used in many forms, such as incense, oils, or sachets. When selecting herbs, consider not only their magical properties but also what they mean to you personally. The scent of an herb can evoke memories and emotions, which can be powerful allies in your spellcasting.

The Significance of Tools in Spells

Each tool you choose should have a clear purpose and significance to your spell. They are not merely accessories; they are symbols of your will and serve to focus your mind on your intentions. For example, when casting a love spell, a rose quartz crystal can be a powerful tool because it is believed to resonate with the heart's desires.

The tools you choose also serve to connect you with the different elements. A bowl of water can represent the emotional realm, a lit candle can signify the transformative power of fire, a feather can symbolize intellect and air, and a crystal or stone can embody the grounding energy of earth.

Integrating Tools into Your Spell

When you have selected your tools, it is important to cleanse them of any previous energies. This can be done through smoke cleansing, burying them in the earth, leaving them out in the moonlight, or any other method that resonates with you.

As you integrate the tools into your spell, do so with intention. As you light your candle, may it light the way for your desires. As you hold your crystal, let it amplify your intention. As you crush your herbs, let their fragrance lift your wishes to the heavens.

Remember, the tools you choose are extensions of your intention. Treat them with respect and care, and they will serve you well in your magical practice. With the right tools in hand, your spells will have the focus and the force to weave change into the fabric of your reality.

Creating Sacred Space

Creating a sacred space is an essential part of spellcasting. It is here where you will commune with the energies of the universe, focus your intentions, and perform your magical work. This space becomes your personal sanctuary, a physical representation of your inner world and your connection to the divine.

Selecting and Cleansing Your Space

Your sacred space can be anywhere you feel comfortable and uninterrupted. It could be a corner of a room, a spot in your garden, or even a portable box you can open when needed. The key is that this space should feel safe and hold a sense of peace for you.

Before you begin using an area for spell work, it must be cleansed of all residual energies. You can cleanse your space by burning herbs like sage, palo santo, or sweetgrass. As the smoke wafts through the area, envision it carrying away all negativity. Alternatively, sound is an excellent cleanser; ringing a bell or playing a singing bowl can also clear the space energetically.

Consecrating Your Space

Once cleansed, it's time to consecrate your space, dedicating it to your magical work. You might choose to say a prayer, chant, or express an invocation to the elements or your chosen deities, asking for their blessing and protection. You could also sprinkle salt water around the area, or trace a pentacle in the air with your finger or a wand.

Setting Up an Altar

Your altar is the focal point of your sacred space. This can be a table, shelf, or any flat surface where you will place items that are significant to your practice. You might include representations of the elements (a candle for fire, a cup of water, a feather for air, and a stone or crystal for earth), images or statues of deities, and any other tools you feel drawn to use in your spells.

Casting Circles

Casting a circle is a powerful way to protect and contain the energy you raise during your spell work. To cast a circle, stand in the center of your sacred space and envision a boundary of energy being drawn around you. You can physically mark this boundary with salt, stones, or crystals if you wish. As you cast your circle, call upon the elements, the cardinal directions, or any guides to watch over and protect the space. This circle acts as a barrier to any unwanted influences and keeps your energy focused.

Your sacred space and altar are living parts of your practice, changing with your needs and the seasons. Treat them with reverence, and they will become allies in your magical work. In this space, you are the conduit between the mundane and the magical, the earthly and the divine. Here, within the circle you have cast, your spells will come to life.

Timing Your Spell

In the craft of spellcasting, timing can be as crucial as the spell itself. Aligning your magical workings with the rhythms of the cosmos can significantly enhance their effectiveness. The phases of the moon, the days of the week, and the turning of the seasons are all powerful allies when timed correctly with your intentions.

Moon Phases

The moon is a potent force in spellcasting and governs the flow of energy much like it governs the tides. Each phase of the moon offers a different energy:

- **New Moon**: The new moon is a time for beginnings, setting intentions, and starting fresh. It's the perfect time to cast spells related to new ventures, such as starting a new job or project.
- **Waxing Moon**: As the moon grows, so does the energy for building and attracting things to you. This is the time for spells that involve increase, such as gaining love, wealth, or success.
- **Full Moon**: The full moon is the peak of magical energy and is suitable for almost any kind of spell. It's particularly potent for spells that require extra power, such as major healing or protection work.
- **Waning Moon**: When the moon is diminishing, it's a period for banishing and releasing. Use this time for spells to get rid of bad habits, toxic energy, or negative influences.

- **Dark Moon**: The period just before the new moon is a time for introspection, divination, and dealing with the shadow self. It's not typically a time for active spellcasting but rather for preparation and understanding.

Days of the Week

Each day of the week is ruled by a different planet and carries its own energy:

- **Sunday (Sun)**: Success, happiness, and health.
- **Monday (Moon)**: Intuition, dreams, and psychic awareness.
- **Tuesday (Mars)**: Courage, conflict resolution, and physical strength.
- **Wednesday (Mercury)**: Communication, study, and travel.
- **Thursday (Jupiter)**: Prosperity, luck, and expansion.
- **Friday (Venus)**: Love, friendship, and beauty.
- **Saturday (Saturn)**: Protection, banishing, and clearing obstacles.

Seasonal Influences

The Wheel of the Year turns through seasons, each providing a unique backdrop for your spells:

- **Spring**: A time of growth and renewal, perfect for spells around new beginnings and growth.
- **Summer**: The season of abundance and fertility, ideal for spells of love, prosperity, and protection.
- **Autumn**: A time for reaping what has been sown, focusing on spells of gratitude and assessment.
- **Winter**: The season of rest and reflection, suitable for introspection and divination spells.

Astrological Considerations

The position of the stars and planets can also influence spellcasting. Astrological events, such as retrogrades or alignments, can affect the energy available for your work. For example, it is often advised not to start new ventures when Mercury is retrograde, as communication may be hampered.

Incorporating Timing into Your Spells

To harness these energies, plan your spells around these natural occurrences. Check a lunar calendar, note the days of the week, and be mindful of the changing seasons. Remember, though, that while timing can aid your spell, the most crucial component is your intention. If an urgent situation arises, don't wait for the 'perfect' time—your immediate need and focused intent are powerful enough.

The Elements of a Spell

When you weave a spell, you are crafting a narrative with a beginning, middle, and end. Each part of this narrative serves a purpose in channeling your intention into the world. Understanding the structure of a spell will help you to compose and cast your spells with confidence.

Invocation

The invocation is your opening, the moment you call upon your guides, the elements, deities, ancestors, or the universe itself. It's an invitation to witness your magic and aid in your work. An invocation can be as simple as lighting a candle and asking for the presence of the element of fire, or as elaborate as reciting a poetic plea to a goddess or god. The key is to call with respect and clarity, setting the tone for the sacred work to come.

Statement of Intent

This is the heart of your spell. Your statement of intent is a clear and concise declaration of what you wish to accomplish. It is spoken, chanted, or sometimes written down, and it is always definitive. There's no room for ambiguity here; your words must reflect exactly what you want to achieve, whether it's 'I attract abundance and prosperity' or 'I protect my home from all harm.'

The Action

This is where the energy you've summoned with your invocation and intent is shaped and directed. The action could be mixing herbs, tying knots, placing crystals, anointing a candle, or any number of other ritual acts. Each movement and each object used in this stage is symbolic, contributing to the buildup of energy and the narrative of the spell.

The Closing

Just as important as the opening, the closing of a spell is where you seal the energy you've raised and release it to do your bidding. It's a gesture of completion and trust that the work you've done will manifest the change you desire. You might close your spell with words like 'So mote it be,' 'It is done,' or simply 'Thank you.' Then, you often extinguish candles, dismantle the circle, or take some other action to signify the end of the ritual.

The closing is also where you ground yourself, releasing any excess energy back into the earth, and return to the mundane world, knowing your spell is at work.

Visualization Techniques

Visualization is one of the most powerful mental tools in your spellcasting arsenal. It is the act of vividly imagining your desired outcome coming to fruition. By creating a clear mental image, you are shaping the energy of your intentions and directing it towards your goal. Here are some techniques to enhance your visualization skills, which can profoundly impact the potency of your spells.

Creating a Mind's Eye Image

Begin by closing your eyes and taking several deep breaths to center yourself. With each inhale and exhale, let go of any tension and allow your mind to become more focused. Picture your intention as clearly as you can in your mind. If you're casting a spell for prosperity, see yourself receiving abundance, perhaps visualizing a check with your name on it or a wallet overflowing with money.

Engaging Your Senses

A detailed visualization engages all the senses. Imagine not only what your desired outcome looks like but also what it feels like, sounds like, and even smells or tastes like. If your spell is for a new job, imagine the texture of the handshake as you're offered the position, the sound of your new colleagues welcoming you, the scent of the office, and the celebratory meal you'll have afterwards.

Adding Emotion

The emotional charge behind your visualization is its true power. Feel the joy, excitement, or peace that comes with achieving your goal. The stronger and more genuinely you can feel these emotions during your visualization, the more energy you are giving to your spell.

Practicing Regularly

Like any skill, visualization gets better with practice. Make time each day to practice visualizing different outcomes and sensations. You can do this as part of your daily meditation, before you go to sleep, or whenever you have a quiet moment.

Using Guided Imagery

Sometimes, starting with guided imagery can be helpful. This could involve listening to a recorded visualization meditation or reading a descriptive passage from a book. As you become more adept, you will be able to guide yourself through the process.

Incorporating Visualization into Spell Work

When casting your spell, incorporate these visualization techniques as you perform the actions of your spell. As you light a candle, see the flame as the spark of your intention. When you tie knots in a cord, visualize your goal being bound to you. As you sprinkle herbs or place crystals, picture your desires materializing.

Anchor the Visual with the Physical

Sometimes having a physical object to focus on can help solidify your visualization. This could be a photograph that represents your goal, a model, a drawing, or any item that helps you to keep the image of your intention clear in your mind.

Releasing the Image

After you have raised energy with your visualization, release it as you conclude your spell. Imagine it leaving your body and going out into the universe to manifest. Trust that the energy will return to you, bringing your intention into reality.

Raising and Directing Energy

Energy is the currency of spellcasting, the raw material that you shape and direct to manifest your intentions. Raising and directing this energy is crucial for effective spell work. This energy can come from within you, from the natural world, or from the elements around you. Here's how you can raise and direct energy during your spellcasting.

Grounding and Centering

Before you begin to raise energy, it's important to ground and center yourself. This means establishing a stable and balanced starting point. Grounding connects you with the Earth, drawing up its endless reservoir of energy. You can ground yourself by visualizing roots growing from your feet deep into the Earth, anchoring you and allowing you to draw upon its strength.

Building Personal Energy

To raise your personal energy, focus on your breath and your body. Feel the life force within you. Begin to visualize this energy as a light or a color. As you concentrate on your breath, imagine this energy building and growing stronger with each inhale. Movement and dance, chanting, drumming, or rhythmic clapping can also help to increase your personal energy.

Working with Elemental Energy

Each of the four elements—earth, air, fire, and water—has its own unique energy that can be harnessed in spellcasting. You can call upon these energies and draw them towards you. Visualize the warmth and brightness of fire, the flow and coolness of water, the solidity of earth, and the movement of air. Use corresponding tools (like a candle for fire, a bowl of water, a stone, or a feather) to help you connect with these elemental forces.

Raising Energy with Tools and Symbols

The tools and symbols you use in your spell—herbs, crystals, candles, wands—can all serve as focal points for energy.

As you handle these items, visualize them glowing with potential. Charge them with your intention and see them as active participants in your spell.

Directing the Energy

Once you've raised this energy, it's time to direct it. Focus on your intention and visualize the energy moving towards it. This can be done by pointing a wand, using your hands to direct the flow, or simply by the power of your will. Imagine your intention and the energy you've raised merging into one potent force.

Sealing the Energy

After directing the energy towards your intention, it's important to seal it. This can be done by making a final statement, such as "So mote it be," or by visualizing a seal over the energy, like closing a lid on a jar. This helps to contain and consolidate the energy, ensuring that it goes to work for your intention.

Grounding Excess Energy

After the spell is complete, you may find yourself with excess energy. It's important to ground this energy to avoid feeling jittery or unbalanced. Visualize it flowing back into the Earth or dissipate it by shaking out your limbs, eating something, or visualizing it washing away with water.

Raising and directing energy is a dance between you and the forces of nature. With practice, you will become more adept at sensing energy and moving it with precision. Remember, the energy you work with is an extension of your will and intention—treat it with respect, and it will serve you well in your magical practice.

Words of Power

Words are the vessel through which thoughts and intentions are conveyed. In the realm of spellcasting, they are more than mere communication; they are the incantations that breathe life into your intentions, shaping the energy you raise and directing it toward your purpose. The art of using words of power lies in their selection, their pronunciation, and the emotion and conviction behind them.

Chants and Incantations

A chant or incantation is a set of words repeated over and over to build energy and focus the mind. The repetition is meditative, allowing you to sink deeper into the spell's intent and raise energy with rhythmic consistency. The vibration of the words spoken aloud can resonate through your body and the space around you, harmonizing with the frequencies of your intention.

Writing Your Own Words of Power

Crafting your own words for a spell is a powerful way to personalize your magic. When you create your own incantation, you are infusing the spell with your unique voice and perspective, making it more authentic and potent. Here are some tips for writing your own words of power:

- Start by clearly stating your intention.
- Use positive and affirmative language.
- Keep it simple and easy to remember.
- Incorporate rhyme or rhythm to give it a flow.
- Use powerful and meaningful words that resonate with you.

Using Traditional Incantations

Traditional incantations come with the weight of history and the power of collective belief.

Here are ten examples of incantations, each tailored to a specific intent:

1. **For Love**: "Heart to heart, I call to thee, bring true love and joy to me. As I will, so mote it be."
2. **For Prosperity**: "Abundance flow and riches grow, to me, to stay, as tides ebb and flow."

3. **For Protection**: "By the power of three times three, as I will, so mote it be. Circle round, to guard and bound, protect me now, from all around."

4. **For Healing**: "Heal and mend, repair and tend, restore my strength, my body mend."

5. **For Peace**: "Calm and center, peace enter, serenity be mine, in this moment's time."

6. **For Clarity**: "Fog disperse, clouds now lift, clear my sight, grant me this gift."

7. **For Courage**: "Brave of heart and strong of will, my spirit rises, fears be still."

8. **For Wisdom**: "Ancient wisdom, knowledge clear, come to me, I'm open to hear."

9. **For Banishing Negativity**: "Shadows flee and darkness parts, away from me, protect my heart."

10. **For Happiness**: "Joy and laughter, come to me, as I will, so shall it be."

These incantations have been used and charged with energy by many practitioners over time, which can add to their effectiveness. When using traditional words, it's important to understand their meaning and context fully. Ensure they align with your intention and values, as this alignment empowers the spell.

Activating Words of Power

Whether you're using your own words or traditional ones, the key to activating them as words of power lies in your delivery. Speak with authority and conviction. Visualize the words carrying your intent out into the universe. Feel the energy of the words as you say them, and imagine that energy transforming into the change you wish to see.

Incorporating Words into Your Spell

Incorporate your words of power at the peak of your spell, when your energy is at its highest. This is typically just before you release and direct the energy towards your goal. As you chant or recite your incantation, hold the image of your desired outcome firmly in your mind. Use the energy you've raised to give the words an extra push.

Concluding Your Incantation

As you finish your incantation, signal the end of the spell with a closing word or phrase such as "So mote it be," "As I will it, so shall it be," or simply "Done." This not only marks the end of the spell but also serves as a final affirmation of your intent, releasing the words and their energy to do your bidding.

Sealing the Spell

Once you have raised and directed the energy towards your intention and recited your words of power, it is time to seal the spell. This act is a sacred affirmation, a final stamp that says, "It is done." Sealing the spell ensures that the energy you have crafted is complete, intact, and sent off to do your magical bidding.

To seal a spell, you can use a simple physical gesture, such as joining your hands together, or a statement of closure, like "So mote it be," or "The spell is sealed; let it be real." Some practitioners like to visualize their intentions as light or energy being tied up in a bow, or being locked within a box, signifying the completion of the spell.

You may also choose to extinguish any candles, carefully snuffing them out while envisioning your intent being locked in with the smoke. If you've cast a circle, now is the time to take down your circle, often done by walking in the opposite direction to which it was cast, thanking and releasing any energies or entities that assisted in your workings.

After the Spell

After the spell has been sealed, it is important to ground yourself. This involves releasing any residual energy that may remain within you to prevent the buildup of excess energy, which can sometimes result in feelings of jitteriness or disconnection. You can ground this energy by imagining it flowing out of you and back into the earth, eating grounding foods, or placing your hands on the ground.

Next, take care of any spell remnants. If you have used any biodegradable materials, you may wish to return them to the earth by burying them. Non-biodegradable items should be cleansed and stored for future use, or disposed of respectfully. If your spell included a written component, you might burn or bury the paper, or keep it somewhere safe, depending on the nature of your work.

Finally, take some time to reflect on the spellcasting experience. You might want to write down what you did, how you felt, and any thoughts or insights that arose during the ritual in your Book of Shadows or a journal. This not only serves as a record of your magical practice but can be a helpful reference to track the outcomes and efficacy of your spells.

Remember, the conclusion of your spell is not the end of the magic. It is the beginning of its journey from the realm of intention into the realm of reality. Give your spell time to work and keep your eyes open for signs and changes in alignment with your intentions. Magic is a subtle art, and its manifestations can be gentle whispers rather than thunderous roars. Trust in the process, and know that the universe is conspiring with your will.

CHAPTER 4.
101 MAGIC SPELLS

Welcome to Chapter 4, where the real magic begins. This is where you'll find "101 Magic Spells," a collection that's going to be your trusty guide as you start to explore the world of spellcasting. Think of this chapter as your magical toolbox, packed with a variety of spells for almost every aspect of your daily life.

In these pages, you'll discover spells of all kinds, each with its own purpose and charm. We've got love spells that open the door to romance and deepen connections, and protection spells to keep you safe from negative vibes. Need a financial boost? Try our money spells. If work's got you stressed, our work spells can help you find balance and success. For those looking to strengthen bonds, our friendship spells are perfect. And when it comes to health and forgiveness, we've got you covered with spells that promote healing and let you release old grudges.

You'll also find spells for general well-being, because taking care of your inner self is just as important as managing the world around you. And for those times when you need a little extra luck or resources, our abundance spells are just the ticket.

Each spell in this collection is straightforward and beginner-friendly, so don't worry if you're just starting out. Remember, the most important ingredient in any spell is your intention. So whether you're hoping to attract something new into your life or simply seeking a bit of daily magic, approach each spell with a clear heart and an open mind.

Feel free to tweak these spells to suit your style. Witchcraft is a personal journey, and there's always room to add your own touch. Maybe you'll find a certain herb that speaks to you, or a special chant that resonates with your soul – go ahead and make these spells your own.

So, are you ready to start casting? Let's dive into the world of magic together, one spell at a time. Here's to your journey into spellcasting – may it be as rewarding and as fun as you've imagined!

1. CREATIVITY SIGIL CANDLE SPELL

Intent: To ignite the flame of creativity within you, helping to unblock artistic expression and inspire innovative ideas.

You Will Need:
- A candle (choose orange for creativity, inspiration, and attraction of positive influences)
- A carving tool (a small stick, needle, or anything sharp enough to inscribe the candle)
- Paper and pen
- An essential oil associated with creativity (such as lemon for clarity or peppermint for mental stimulation)
- A quiet space where you will be undisturbed

Preparation:
1. Begin by cleansing your space. You might burn some sage or sweep your area with a feather to clear away any negative energy.
2. Sit in the middle of your space and ground yourself. Visualize roots extending from your body deep into the earth, anchoring you and providing stability.

Crafting Your Sigil:

1. On a piece of paper, write down your creative intention. It could be as simple as "My creativity flows freely and abundantly."

2. Simplify this statement by removing vowels and repeating consonants, leaving you with a string of unique letters.

3. Take these letters and begin to combine them into a symbol or sigil. This is a personal process, so let your intuition guide you.

4. Once satisfied with your sigil, take a moment to charge it with your intention. Hold it in your hands and visualize your creative energy infusing the sigil.

The Spell:

1. Take your candle and carve the sigil into its side with your carving tool. As you carve, focus on the flow of creativity you wish to unlock within yourself.

2. Anoint the candle with a few drops of your chosen essential oil. As you rub the oil into the candle, imagine it being charged with the bright, invigorating energy of creativity.

3. Place the candle in a holder and light it. As the flame catches, visualize it igniting the power of your sigil and your creative energies.

4. Focus on the flame and imagine it growing brighter, its light spreading warmth and energy that begins to swirl around you, filling you with confidence and inspiration.

5. As you concentrate on the flame, repeat the following incantation: "By this sigil, creativity is unbound, Within me, a wellspring of ideas is found. As this candle burns, so does my creative light, Igniting passion, bringing my art to new heights."

Sealing the Spell:

1. Allow the candle to burn as you meditate on your intention. When you feel ready, blow out the candle to release your intention to the universe, saying, "As I will it, so shall it be!"

2. Place the piece of paper with your sigil somewhere you will see it regularly, like your workspace or studio, to remind you of the spell and keep the energy of creativity flowing.

After the Spell:

1. Ground any residual energy by visualizing it flowing back into the earth.

2. Save the candle and relight it whenever you need a boost of creative energy.

3. Note your experience in your journal, paying attention to any bursts of creativity in the following days.

2. MOTIVATION SPELL BOTTLE

Intent: To create a lasting talisman that will inspire motivation and drive, helping to overcome procrastination and boost productivity.

You Will Need:
- A small bottle or jar with a lid or cork
- A piece of paper and a pen
- Herbs associated with motivation, such as basil for focus and drive, bay leaves for success, and peppermint for mental clarity
- Small crystals or stones like carnelian for endurance, clear quartz for clarity, and tiger's eye for courage
- An essential oil for motivation, such as orange or rosemary
- Yellow ribbon or string (yellow is associated with the mind and intellect)

Preparation:
1. Cleanse your workspace and your bottle. Use smoke, sound, or visualization to clear away any energies and set a clean slate for your spell.

2. Center yourself with deep breaths, grounding your energy and focusing your mind on the task at hand.

The Spell:

1. Begin by writing your intention for motivation on the piece of paper. Be specific about the areas in your life where you need this boost.

2. Fold the paper small enough to fit into the bottle and set it aside.

3. Carefully place your chosen herbs into the bottle, focusing on their properties and how they will aid in your goal.

4. Add the small crystals or stones, envisioning each one empowering you with their energetic qualities.

5. Drop a few drops of the essential oil onto the folded paper, allowing its fragrance to imbue your intention with an activating charge.

6. Place the paper into the bottle, letting it absorb the energies of the herbs and stones.

7. Seal the bottle and tie the yellow ribbon or string around it while reciting the following incantation: "Drive and focus, come to me, As I will, so mote it be. Let procrastination flee, Unlock my potential, set it free."

Sealing the Spell:

1. As you tie the final knot in the ribbon or string, visualize the bottle glowing with a bright, motivating energy.

2. Seal the bottle with wax if you wish, locking in the energy.

3. Hold the bottle in your hands and take a few moments to meditate on your intention, feeling the energy of the spell bottle merging with your own.

4. Conclude the spell with a firm, "This motivation is now within me."

After the Spell:

1. Ground any leftover energy by placing your palms flat on the earth or floor, visualizing excess energy flowing away.

2. Place your Motivation Spell Bottle on your desk, in your workspace, or carry it with you to keep the energy of motivation and productivity close.

3. Whenever you feel your motivation waning, hold the bottle, shake it gently, and remind yourself of the intention and energy contained within.

3. GOOD IMPRESSIONS CHARM

Intent: To craft a charm that will aid in creating a positive and lasting impression in social situations, interviews, meetings, or any event where you wish to present your best self.

You Will Need:

- A small charm bag or pouch, preferably in a color associated with communication such as light blue or silver
- Lavender for calmness and eloquence
- Rose petals for favor and affability
- A small piece of lapis lazuli or sodalite, stones known for enhancing communication
- A sprig of rosemary for mental clarity and remembrance
- A personal item, such as a piece of jewelry or a written affirmation of your qualities
- An essential oil blend of bergamot for confidence and spearmint for eloquence
- A white or silver ribbon to bind the charm with purity and clarity of intent

Preparation:

1. Begin by finding a quiet space where you can focus without interruptions. Lay out your materials in front of you.

2. Cleanse your space with your preferred method, be it incense, sound, or visualization, creating a clean slate for your intentions.

The Spell:

1. Take the charm bag in your hands and hold it to your heart. Breathe deeply and center yourself, gathering your thoughts on the impression you wish to create.

2. One by one, add the herbs to the bag. As you add the lavender, envision your words flowing smoothly and your demeanor calm and composed. With the rose petals, imagine yourself surrounded by a warm, inviting aura that draws others in.

3. Place the stone into the bag. Feel the stone's weight as an anchor that will keep you centered and articulate during your interactions.

4. Lay the sprig of rosemary atop the contents, allowing its scent to remind you of your purpose and to keep your mind sharp.

5. Add your personal item, infusing the charm with your unique energy and essence.

6. Lastly, anoint the outside of the bag with a drop of the essential oil blend. As you do, say: "With oil, I bless this charm of mine, For grace and ease in every line. May my impressions be bright and clear, To open doors and bring good cheer."

Sealing the Spell:

1. Draw the strings of the charm bag tight and secure them with the white or silver ribbon. As you tie it, visualize sealing your intention within, and say: "This charm is sealed, the spell is cast, A good impression that will last."

2. Hold the completed charm bag between your palms, warming it with your energy and reaffirming your intention.

After the Spell:

1. Ground any residual energy from the spell by taking a few deep breaths, visualizing any excess flowing out of you and into the earth.

2. Carry the Good Impressions Charm with you in situations where you wish to be at your best. It can be tucked into a pocket, worn around the neck, or simply held for a moment before entering the event.

3. After its use, return the charm to your sacred space, giving thanks for its support and for the confidence it has provided.

4. Reflect on your experiences with the charm in your journal. Note any shifts in your interactions and the reception you receive from others, acknowledging the role of your own energies and the support of the charm.

4. ANTI-PROCRASTINATION OIL

Intent: To create a magical oil blend that spurs motivation, wards off the heavy cloak of procrastination, and invites a steady flow of energy for productivity.

You Will Need:

- A small, dark glass bottle to preserve the oil's potency
- A base oil, such as sweet almond or jojoba, to carry the essence of the herbs
- Essential oils associated with focus and action, such as:
- Lemon for clarity and concentration
- Rosemary for mental power and banishing mental fatigue
- Black pepper for courage and overcoming mental blockages
- A small piece of pyrite or clear quartz, to amplify focus and intention
- A label and pen to mark the bottle with your intentions

Preparation:

1. Choose a quiet and comfortable space to work, where you feel most at ease to focus on your intentions.

2. Begin with a cleansing ritual to purify your space and materials, ensuring that no lingering energies will interfere with your blend.

The Spell:

1. Start by filling your bottle halfway with your chosen base oil.

2. As you add each essential oil, envision each drop dispersing procrastination and infusing the carrier oil with powerful, motivating energy. Begin with lemon, saying, "Lemon bright, clear the mind, cut through confusion, clarity find."

3. Add rosemary next, with the words, "Rosemary strong, protect my thoughts, sustain my focus, tie no knots."

4. Follow with black pepper, chanting, "Black pepper bold, banish fear, strengthen will, bring drive near."

5. Each time you add an oil, gently swirl the bottle to mix the oils, visualizing them blending their energies harmoniously.

6. Once all essential oils have been added, place the pyrite or clear quartz into the bottle. Seal it tightly, and as you do, say, "Stone of power, in you lies, strength to conquer, all that ties."

7. Label the bottle with a name that embodies the blend's purpose, like "Momentum" or "Flow Force Oil."

Sealing the Spell:

1. Hold the sealed oil bottle in both hands and close your eyes. Take deep breaths and with each exhale, imagine any feelings of delay or lethargy leaving your body.

2. Speak the final words, "This oil is charged, the spell is made, no more to wait, nor to evade."

3. Shake the bottle gently to finalize the blending of oils and intentions.

After the Spell:

1. Ground yourself by touching the earth or floor with your hands, releasing any excess energy.

2. Store the Anti-Procrastination Oil in a cool, dark place until you're ready to use it.

3. When it's time to work, dab a small amount of the oil on your wrists, temples, or other pulse points, and inhale deeply to let its aroma invigorate your senses and your determination.

4. As you use the oil, make a note of your progress and productivity levels, reflecting on the blend's

effectiveness and your personal growth in your magical diary.

With your Anti-Procrastination Oil, you now have a quick and easy ritual aid to help clear the mind, energize your spirit, and keep you steadfast on the path to accomplishment.

5. CLEARING A PATH SPELL

Intent: To remove obstacles and clear the way for success and progress in any aspect of your life where you feel blocked or hindered.

You Will Need:

- A white candle for purity and new beginnings
- A pathway-clearing herb such as eucalyptus, pine, or cedar
- A small clear quartz crystal to amplify your intentions
- A piece of paper and pen
- A fire-safe bowl or dish

Preparation:

1. Find a quiet place where you can perform the spell without interruption.
2. Cleanse your space, tools, and ingredients to ensure there's no residual energy that could interfere with your work.

The Spell:

1. Sit comfortably and take a few deep breaths to center yourself. Light the white candle and focus

on its flame, letting it symbolize the clarity and openness you seek.

2. On the piece of paper, write down the specific obstacles you wish to overcome. These could be internal, like fear or self-doubt, or external, such as a specific situation that is impeding your progress.

3. Once you've finished writing, fold the paper away from you, symbolically pushing the obstacles out of your path.

4. Lay the folded paper in your fire-safe bowl or dish.

5. Sprinkle the pathway-clearing herb over the paper. As you do so, say, "Herbs of power, herbs so clear, remove obstructions, far and near."

6. Place the clear quartz crystal atop the paper and herbs, and say, "Quartz so clear, amplify my intent, let my path be free of dent."

7. Carefully, light the paper on fire, allowing the herbs and the words written on the paper to burn. As they turn to ash, visualize your obstacles disintegrating, and imagine a clear path opening before you.

8. While the paper burns, say: "What blocks my way now turns to dust, Make clear my path, in this I trust. Obstacles burn, to ash they fall, Open the road, I conquer all."

Sealing the Spell:

1. Watch the paper and herbs turn to ash, releasing your intent to the universe. Once the fire has safely burned out, and the ashes have cooled, say, "The way is clear, the path is bright, nothing can stop my guided light."

2. Extinguish the candle safely, signifying the end of the ritual.

After the Spell:

1. Dispose of the ash by scattering it to the wind, or washing it away with running water, symbolizing the removal of obstacles.

2. Keep the quartz crystal on your person or in a place where you will see it daily as a reminder of your clear path.

3. Ground yourself to balance the energies by eating, touching the earth, or resting.

4. In the following days, keep an eye out for opportunities and signs that your path is becoming clear. Make sure to take proactive steps in the physical world to complement your magical workings.

5. Document your experiences, how you feel after the spell, and any changes that occur in your journal.

Reflect on the efficacy of your spellwork and how it may be guiding you towards success.

This Clearing a Path Spell is a powerful way to assert your will over the stumbling blocks in your life, creating space for new growth and progress.

6. RESPONSIBILITY SPELL

Intent: To cultivate a sense of responsibility and discipline, especially when you need to tackle important tasks or commitments.

You Will Need:

- A small terra cotta pot or a plantable container
- Soil, rich and ready for planting
- Seeds of a plant that symbolizes growth and personal development, such as a sturdy herb like thyme or basil
- A green candle for growth and commitment
- A piece of paper and a pen
- A small piece of malachite or green aventurine to foster responsibility and focus

Preparation:

1. Set up a quiet space where you can focus on the spell without distractions.
2. Cleanse the area, the pot, the candle, and the stone with your preferred method, setting a pure intention for their use.

The Spell:

1. Begin by grounding yourself. Take deep breaths and visualize roots extending from your feet deep into the earth, stabilizing and centering you.

2. Write down the areas of your life where you need to take on more responsibility on the piece of paper. Phrase these in an affirmative way, such as, "I successfully manage my finances," or "I dedicate time to my family."

3. Place the piece of paper at the bottom of the pot, affirming your commitment to grow in these areas.

4. Fill the pot with soil, planting your seeds carefully. As you cover them with earth, visualize each seed representing a commitment you are nurturing.

5. Place the malachite or green aventurine in the soil with the seeds. As you do so, say, "Stone of growth, stone of power, strengthen my will hour by hour."

6. Light the green candle, and as it burns, focus on the flame. Imagine it representing the life force and energy you will put into your responsibilities.

7. Say the following incantation: "From seed to sprout, from sprout to tree, I welcome responsibility. With steady hand and open heart, I commit to do my part."

Sealing the Spell:

1. Watch the candle for a few moments, visualizing your responsibilities being handled with ease and grace.

2. When ready, carefully extinguish the candle, affirming that your intent is set.

3. Water the seeds gently, feeling your commitments being nurtured and beginning to grow.

After the Spell:

1. Place the pot in a space where you will see it daily as a living reminder of your spell and growing responsibilities.

2. As the plant grows, so too will your sense of responsibility. Care for the plant as you would your own tasks—water it, give it sunlight, and keep it healthy.

3. Whenever you attend to the plant, remember the growth you are fostering in your own life.

4. Record your progress and any thoughts or feelings about your growing sense of responsibility in your journal.

This Responsibility Spell helps anchor the intention to be more accountable and disciplined, using the growth of the plant as a mirror for your personal development.

7. BOOSTING PRODUCTIVITY SPELL

Intent: To enhance focus and efficiency, allowing for a more productive mindset and the successful completion of tasks.

You Will Need:
- A blue candle for focus and mental clarity
- A small dish or holder for the candle
- An essential oil blend of peppermint and eucalyptus for mental stimulation and clearing away mental fog
- A clear quartz point to amplify intentions and energies
- A piece of paper and a pen
- A small sachet or fabric square and ribbon to create a productivity pouch

Preparation:
1. Choose a quiet space where you can work undisturbed.
2. Cleanse your space and materials with your preferred method, setting a clean and focused foundation for your spell.

The Spell:

1. Ground yourself by taking deep breaths, feeling a sense of calm and collected energy grounding you to the present moment.

2. Write a list of your specific productivity goals on the piece of paper. Be clear and concise, focusing on what you need to accomplish in the short term.

3. Anoint the blue candle with the essential oil blend, spreading the oil from the base to the wick as you focus on your intent to increase productivity.

4. Place the candle in its holder and light it, watching the flame catch and grow, visualizing it burning away any distractions or procrastination.

5. Hold the clear quartz point in your hands, and visualize it filling with the light of the candle, energizing it with your desire to be productive. Place it near the candle's base.

6. Fold the paper with your goals written on it and place it in the sachet or fabric square. Add any small items that represent productivity to you, such as a small clock charm, a sprig of rosemary, or a tiny scroll symbolizing a to-do list.

7. Gather the corners of the sachet or fabric square and tie it with the ribbon while reciting the following

incantation: "Focus and clarity, now come to me, Efficiency be mine, so mote it be. As this candle burns, so does my drive, With productivity, I now thrive."

Sealing the Spell:

1. Let the candle burn safely in your workspace while you begin working on your tasks, or if it's not safe to leave the candle unattended, watch it for a few moments and then carefully snuff it out, affirming, "My productivity burns as bright as this flame."

2. Carry the productivity pouch with you when working, or keep it in your workspace where you can see it, to draw upon the energy of the spell.

3. Whenever you feel your focus waning, hold the pouch, feeling the textures of its contents, and remember the clarity and drive you infused into it.

After the Spell:

1. Ground any excess energy from the spell by visualizing it flowing into the earth.

2. Reflect on the spell's effectiveness each time you work, noting any increase in productivity or ease in accomplishing tasks in your journal.

3. Recharge the sachet periodically by placing it near a burning candle, or in sunlight, while reaffirming your intent to remain productive.

This Boosting Productivity Spell is designed to create a tangible reminder of your commitment to efficiency and to help maintain a clear, focused mindset for completing your tasks.

8. SELF-LOVE BATH

Intent: To nurture self-acceptance and love, to soothe the spirit, and to encourage a kinder, more compassionate relationship with oneself.

You Will Need:

- A bathtub filled with warm water
- Epsom salts or sea salt for cleansing and purification
- Rose petals or rosewater, for love and acceptance
- Lavender buds or essential oil for calm and balance
- A pink candle for self-love and harmony
- Amethyst or rose quartz crystals for emotional healing and to foster self-love
- Soft, soothing music or sounds (optional)

Preparation:

1. Begin by cleaning the bathroom to create a peaceful and inviting space.
2. Ensure privacy and a time when you will not be interrupted.

The Spell:

1. Draw a warm bath to a comfortable temperature that will soothe and envelop you.

2. As the tub fills, add Epsom salts or sea salt, envisioning them purifying the water and creating a space of healing and renewal.

3. Sprinkle in the rose petals or pour in rosewater, inviting the essence of love into your bath.

4. Add lavender buds or drops of lavender oil to the water for tranquility and to balance your emotions.

5. Carefully place the amethyst or rose quartz crystals around the edge of the bathtub or into the water, where they can infuse the bath with their calming energies.

6. Light the pink candle and set it in a safe place near the bath. As you light it, focus on igniting the flame of self-love within you.

7. If you choose, play some soft, soothing music or nature sounds to aid in relaxation and to create an atmosphere of serenity.

8. Step into the bath, ease your body into the water, and allow yourself to relax fully. Close your eyes and take several deep, cleansing breaths.

9. As you soak, recite the following incantation, either aloud or in your mind: "Waters of love, soak through to my core, With every drop, I love myself more. Heal my heart, set my spirit free, As I will, so mote it be."

Sealing the Spell:

1. Soak in the bath for as long as you need, feeling the loving energies enveloping you.
2. When ready to emerge, visualize any negative self-perceptions washing away, leaving only love and acceptance.
3. Extinguish the candle safely, affirming the warmth of self-love that now burns steadily within you.

After the Bath:

1. Drain the tub and imagine any remaining self-doubt or negativity flowing away with the water.
2. As you dry off, be gentle with yourself, as if with the touch of a loving hand.
3. Wrap yourself in a comfortable robe or towel and spend some time in quiet reflection, acknowledging the love you have for yourself.
4. Journal about your experience, noting the sensations, thoughts, and emotions that arose during the bath.

This Self-Love Bath is a sacred ritual to remind you of your worth and to reinforce a nurturing and compassionate attitude towards yourself.

9. ROSE ATTRACTION POTION

Intent: To create a potion that enhances personal charm and allure, drawing positive attention and affection towards oneself.

You Will Need:

- A small bottle or vial with a secure cap
- Rose water for its loving and attraction properties
- Fresh rose petals, preferably from red roses for passion or pink for gentle love
- A small piece of vanilla pod or a few drops of vanilla extract for warmth and welcoming energy
- Honey for sweetening interactions and relationships
- Cinnamon for quick and passionate attraction
- A small rose quartz crystal to charge the potion with loving energy
- A piece of parchment paper and a pen

Preparation:

1. Choose a time and space where you won't be disturbed, ideally on a Friday as it's the day of Venus, the planet of love.

2.   Cleanse your space and ingredients energetically to ensure they're imbued only with your current intent.

The Spell:

1.   Begin by focusing on your intent for attraction and what kind of attention you wish to draw. Write this down on the parchment paper.

2.   Place the rose quartz crystal in your potion bottle. As you do this, visualize the stone's energy radiating out, attracting love and warmth.

3.   Pour the rose water into the bottle, filling it to about halfway. As you pour, chant softly, "Waters of love, bring attraction near, draw to me those I hold dear."

4.   Add the rose petals, vanilla, a dollop of honey, and a pinch of cinnamon. With each ingredient, say a line that corresponds to its property, such as "Rose for love, vanilla for warmth, honey for sweetness, cinnamon for charm."

5.   Seal the bottle and shake it gently, mixing the ingredients as you focus on creating a magnetic and inviting aura around you.

6.   Hold the bottle between your hands, close your eyes, and visualize a soft, pink light enveloping you, emanating from the potion and drawing in affection and positive attention.

7. Recite the following incantation: "This potion of attraction is now complete, Bringing forth affection sweet. Charm and grace are now my plea, As I will, so mote it be."

Sealing the Spell:

1. Seal the parchment paper with your written intent by passing it through the candle flame carefully and allowing it to catch fire. Place it in a fireproof dish to burn safely.

2. As the paper turns to ash, understand that your intention is released into the universe, solidifying your will.

3. Store the potion in a place where it can continue to charge, such as on a windowsill bathed in moonlight or a special altar.

After the Spell:

1. When you wish to exude an aura of attraction, dab the potion on your pulse points or add a few drops to your bath water.

2. Dispose of the ash from the parchment paper by scattering it to the wind or burying it in the earth.

3. Ground yourself by enjoying a moment of stillness, a sweet treat, or a few deep breaths, releasing any excess energy from the spell.

4. Document your potion-making experience and any effects you notice when using your Rose Attraction Potion in your magical journal.

This potion, imbued with your intent and the energies of attraction, is now ready to assist you in gracefully drawing the attention and affection you desire.

10. COME TO ME OIL

Intent: To create a magnetic oil that draws a specific person or opportunity closer to you, in accordance with your highest good and theirs.

You Will Need:

- A base oil, like sweet almond or jojoba, as the carrier for your intentions
- Jasmine essential oil for love and prophetic dreams
- Orange essential oil for attraction and joy
- Patchouli essential oil for grounding and manifestation
- A small cinnamon stick or a pinch of cinnamon powder for warmth and speed
- A tiny magnet or magnetic sand to symbolize attraction
- A small bottle or vial to blend and hold your oil
- A label and pen to mark your creation

Preparation:

1. Find a quiet and comfortable space where you can work undisturbed.

2. Cleanse your space, materials, and self to ensure there's no residual energy that might affect the purity of your intention.

The Spell:

1. Center yourself with a few deep breaths, grounding your energy and focusing on the person or opportunity you wish to attract.
2. Fill your bottle halfway with the base oil.
3. Begin by adding a few drops of jasmine essential oil while saying, "Jasmine, draw my love to me, as I will it, so it shall be."
4. Add a few drops of orange essential oil, invoking its sunny power with the words, "Orange bright, attract what's right, bring (person/opportunity) into my sight."
5. Next, incorporate patchouli essential oil with the intention, "Patchouli deep, secure my plea, draw (person/opportunity) close to me."
6. If using a cinnamon stick, place it into the bottle; if using powder, sprinkle it in gently. As you do so, chant, "Cinnamon warm, bring swift form, to my will, this bond be born."
7. Add the magnet or magnetic sand to the bottle, affirming, "As iron to magnet, draw near what I seek, in harmony and truth, not through force or pique."

8. Seal the bottle and gently roll it between your palms to blend the oils, warming them with your hands and further charging them with your energy.

9. While holding the bottle, visualize the person or opportunity being drawn to you irresistibly, as if pulled by the force of the magnet within your oil.

10. Conclude your spell with the words, "This Come to Me Oil is now made, a potent charm that will not fade. By this blend, my call is heard, in alignment with the Word."

Sealing the Spell:

1. Affix the label to your bottle, naming your Come to Me Oil. This acts as a final seal on your magical work, tying the physical and the metaphysical together.

2. Place the bottle in a spot where you can see it daily or keep it with your other magical tools until you're ready to use it.

After the Spell:

1. Anoint candles, charms, or yourself with the oil when working towards drawing your desired person or opportunity.

2. Ground yourself by eating something hearty, placing your feet firmly on the ground, or engaging in another act of self-care.

3. Reflect on the process and document any signs, dreams, or synchronicities that occur after using the oil in your journal.

Your Come to Me Oil is now ready to use, charged with the energies of attraction and connection, to be used mindfully and with respect for the free will of all parties involved.

11. DESIRE INCENSE

Intent: To craft an incense blend that ignites passion and desire, either in the context of self-love or within a consensual romantic relationship.

You Will Need:

- Dried rose petals for love and attraction
- Damiana leaf for enhancing passion and desire
- Vanilla bean or vanilla pods for sweetness and warmth
- Cinnamon for quick action and heating up emotions
- Sandalwood powder or chips for its sensual and inviting aroma
- A mortar and pestle for blending and grinding your herbs
- Charcoal discs for burning your incense
- A fireproof incense burner or dish

Preparation:

1. Create a space conducive to focus and intention. You may wish to perform this spell on a Friday, Venus's day, which corresponds with love and desire.

2. Cleanse your ingredients and tools, as well as your space, to ensure that your incense is charged only with your current intentions.

The Spell:

1. Ground yourself to begin, envisioning your energy connecting deeply with the earth, providing a stable foundation for your work.

2. Take the dried rose petals in your hands, feeling their texture, and as you add them to the mortar, say, "Petals of rose, ignite the flame, draw forth passion, in Venus's name."

3. Add damiana leaf, known for its affinity with sexual desire and attraction. As you crumble the leaves, chant, "Damiana, herb of fire, stoke within me ardent desire."

4. Scrape the seeds from the vanilla pod or add a piece of vanilla bean, invoking its essence with, "Vanilla, sweet and warm, bring to me a love that's sworn."

5. Sprinkle in cinnamon, for an immediate and passionate spark, saying, "Cinnamon, spice of speed, bring the desire that I need."

6. Lastly, mix in sandalwood, with its earthy and seductive scent, while reciting, "Sandalwood, draw what I seek, through smoke, this passion peaks."

7. Grind the mixture in your mortar and pestle, blending all the ingredients until they are a coarse powder. As you grind, focus on the qualities of desire you wish to manifest, visualizing the incense carrying your intentions on its smoke as it burns.

8. When the blend is ready, light a charcoal disc in your incense burner until it's glowing red and sprinkle a pinch of your Desire Incense on top.

9. As the incense begins to smolder and the aromatic smoke rises, say: "By this scented smoke, desire is freed, Drawn to me, in thought and deed. As it burns, so kindle true, The fires of passion, bright and new."

Sealing the Spell:

1. Watch the smoke as it drifts upwards, carrying your intentions out into the universe.

2. When you feel the time is right, conclude your ritual by saying, "My will is sent, the spell is cast, draw to me a love that lasts."

3. Allow the charcoal to burn out naturally, ensuring it's completely extinguished before disposing of it safely.

After the Spell:

1. Store any leftover incense in a jar or bag, labeling it with its purpose and the date of creation.
2. Ground yourself again, perhaps by eating something or spending time in nature.
3. Keep a record of when you use the incense and any feelings or experiences that arise, noting these in your journal.

Your Desire Incense is now ready to be used whenever you wish to create an atmosphere charged with passion and longing.

12. SWEET DREAMS SACHET

Intent: To foster peaceful, restful sleep and encourage positive, healing dreams.

You Will Need:
- A small fabric pouch or sachet, preferably in calming colors like blue or lavender
- Dried lavender buds for relaxation and peace
- Dried chamomile flowers for their sleep-inducing properties
- Dried rose petals to inspire positive and loving dreams
- A small piece of amethyst for its tranquil energy and ability to promote peaceful sleep
- A few drops of lavender or chamomile essential oil for added calm
- A small slip of paper and a pen
- A ribbon or string to tie the sachet closed

Preparation:
1. Find a quiet space where you can concentrate on crafting your sachet.

2. Cleanse your space and materials with your preferred method to create a serene and pure setting for your intentions.

The Spell:

1. Center yourself with deep, slow breaths, allowing the quiet of the moment to settle over you like a soft blanket.

2. On the slip of paper, write down an affirmation for your sleep, such as, "I enjoy deep, restorative sleep and awaken feeling refreshed."

3. Place the slip of paper in the bottom of the sachet. This will serve as the foundation of your intentions.

4. Begin to fill the sachet with the dried herbs. As you add the lavender, say, "Lavender, herb of peace, bring me calm that does not cease."

5. Add the chamomile, and speak, "Chamomile, gentle and mild, grant me rest like a child."

6. As you sprinkle in the rose petals, say, "Roses sweet, with dreams so fair, fill my night with love, not care."

7. Place the amethyst in the sachet, with the words, "Amethyst, stone of night, ease my mind till morning light."

8. Add a few drops of essential oil to the herbs, not directly on the paper, and gently shake the sachet to distribute the scent.

9. Draw the edges of the sachet together and tie it closed with the ribbon or string. As you secure the knot, say, "This sachet is sealed, the magic cast, sweet dreams are mine, from first to last."

Sealing the Spell:

1. Hold the completed sachet in your hands, gently squeezing it to release the scents. Take a deep breath in, letting the aroma soothe you, and as you exhale, visualize any tension or worry leaving your body.

2. Say a final affirmation, such as, "Now I lay me down to sleep, into dreams, sweet and deep."

3. Place the sachet under your pillow, within your pillowcase, or on your bedside table.

After the Spell:

1. As you lay down to sleep, feel the presence of the sachet as a source of comfort and peace.

2. When you wake, take a moment to recall your dreams and feelings upon awakening, jotting them down in a dream journal.

3. Regularly refresh the sachet with new herbs and
    oils, and recharge the amethyst under moonlight to
    maintain the sachet's potency.

Your Sweet Dreams Sachet is now a gentle talisman, ready
to accompany you into the world of dreams, ensuring that
your nighttime hours are as restorative and magical as they
can be.

13. NEW HOME PURIFICATION

Intent: To cleanse and bless a new living space, to remove any negative energy left by previous occupants, and to fill the home with positivity, protection, and harmony.

You Will Need:

- A white candle for purity and new beginnings
- Sea salt or Himalayan salt for purification
- Sage, palo santo, or cedar for smudging and cleansing
- A small bowl of water infused with lemon or orange peels for freshness and joy
- Essential oil of lavender or rosemary for peace and protection
- A bell or chime to break up old energy patterns
- A loaf of bread and a new coin for abundance and sustenance

Preparation:

1. Open all windows and doors to allow fresh air and energy to circulate.
2. Clean the physical space thoroughly, as physical cleanliness assists in spiritual cleansing.
3. Prepare your cleansing tools and have them easily accessible as you move through the space.

The Spell:

1. Light the white candle, setting it in a central area of the home, and focus on the flame representing a new start, illuminating the home with positive light.

2. Walk to each corner of every room and sprinkle a pinch of salt, saying, "Salt that cleanses, protect this space, and let no negativity remain in this place."

3. Begin smudging with your choice of sage, palo santo, or cedar. As the smoke wafts through the rooms, chant, "Smoke of sage (or palo santo/cedar), clear and pure, cleanse this home, let peace endure."

4. Take the bowl of water, dip your fingers in, and flick droplets in each room, saying, "Water with lemon (or orange), clean and bright, wash away all but light."

5. Anoint the doorframes and windowsills with a drop of lavender or rosemary oil for ongoing protection, with the words, "Oil of lavender (or rosemary), guard this place, secure our home, our peaceful base."

6. Ring the bell or chime as you walk through each room to break up any stagnant energy, repeating, "Ring for harmony, ring for peace, with each chime, may blessings increase."

Sealing the Spell:

1. When you have moved through each space, return to the candle. Place the loaf of bread and new coin

near it, symbolizing abundance and prosperity in your new home.

2. Say, "Bread for sustenance, coin for wealth, within these walls, let there be health."

3. Blow out the candle, visualizing the smoke carrying your intentions throughout the home.

4. Close all windows and doors, symbolically sealing in the new energy.

After the Spell:

1. Enjoy a piece of the bread, sharing it with those who dwell in the home, as you collectively welcome the energy of abundance and well-being.

2. Place the coin in a common area of the home, such as on a mantle or in a jar, to attract prosperity.

3. Reflect on the process and how the space feels now, taking note of any changes in the atmosphere or your feelings about the new living space.

4. Maintain the purity and harmony of the space with regular cleanings, both physical and spiritual, and by placing protective symbols or plants in key areas.

Your New Home Purification spell is complete, setting the foundation for a peaceful, harmonious, and prosperous dwelling.

14. HEALING MOON TALISMAN

Intent: To create a talisman that harnesses the healing energy of the moon, intended to promote physical, emotional, and spiritual well-being.

You Will Need:

- A small cloth pouch or a piece of blue or silver fabric and ribbon to create a pouch
- Moonstone or selenite crystal for connection to lunar energy and healing
- A white candle to represent the moon's healing light
- Dried lavender or eucalyptus for their healing properties
- A piece of paper and a pen
- A small silver coin to represent the moon
- Lavender or eucalyptus essential oil for additional healing properties

Preparation:

1. Choose a time to perform this spell when the moon is visible, ideally when it is full or waxing for increasing health.

2. Cleanse your space and all items with your preferred method to ensure they carry only your energy and intentions.

The Spell:

1. Begin by lighting the white candle, focusing on the clean, healing flame as a symbol of the moon's pure light.

2. Hold the moonstone or selenite crystal in your hand, and in the light of the candle, charge it with your intention for healing. Say, "Stone of the moon, bless me with healing, as above, so below, let this be my sealing."

3. Write your specific healing intentions on the piece of paper. Fold it toward you to bring the healing energy in.

4. Place the folded paper in the center of the fabric, or open the cloth pouch.

5. Add the dried lavender or eucalyptus on top of the paper, and as you do so, chant, "Herbs of healing, sooth and repair, bring to me your tender care."

6. Place the silver coin in the pouch, affirming, "As the moon travels the night sky, so too shall my healing rise."

7. Add a drop of the essential oil to the herbs, and say, "Oil of purity, with healing so true, I infuse you with light, a balm for the blue."

8. Place the charged crystal in the pouch, and then draw the fabric together and tie it with the ribbon, or close the pouch. As you secure the talisman, visualize sealing the healing energies inside.

9. Hold the completed talisman in both hands and say, "By the moon's light and the stars above, I activate this talisman with love. To heal, to soothe, to mend and restore, with each phase, I feel better, more and more."

Sealing the Spell:

1. Snuff out the candle, envisioning the healing intentions spreading out into the universe.

2. If outside, hold the talisman up to the moon, allowing it to bathe in the moonlight, further charging it with luminous energy.

After the Spell:

1. Keep the Healing Moon Talisman with you, especially during times when you need a boost in healing energy.

2. Place it under your pillow at night to tap into the restorative powers of sleep and the moon.

3. Regularly recharge your talisman by placing it in the moonlight on clear nights, especially during the full or waxing phases.

4. Note any changes in your health or well-being, and journal about your experiences with the talisman.

This Healing Moon Talisman now serves as a personal healing companion, imbued with the nurturing energies of the moon and the earth.

15. BODY VITALITY BUTTER

Intent: To craft a luxurious body butter that not only moisturizes the skin but also infuses the body with energy and vitality.

You Will Need:

- A base butter, such as shea butter or cocoa butter, for nourishment and smoothness
- Coconut oil for its hydrating and revitalizing properties
- A few drops of ginger essential oil for its warming and energizing effects
- A few drops of peppermint essential oil for invigoration and mental clarity
- A few drops of orange essential oil for cheerfulness and an energy boost
- A glass jar or container for storing your body butter
- A mixing bowl and mixer (or a whisk)

Preparation:

1. Find a calm time when you can create your body butter without interruptions.

2. Cleanse your space, tools, and ingredients to make sure that your body butter is imbued only with positive energy.

The Spell:

1. Begin by grounding yourself, breathing deeply, and centering your energy.

2. In your mixing bowl, start with a generous scoop of your base butter. As you add it, say, "Butter of the earth, rich and pure, imbue my skin with health, that's sure."

3. Add a spoonful of coconut oil, stating, "Oil of the coconut, lend me your vigor, for energy in abundance, and strength in figure."

4. As you drop in the ginger essential oil, chant, "Ginger so fiery, warm my essence, grant me your zest and effervescent presence."

5. With the addition of peppermint essential oil, say, "Peppermint crisp, clear my mind, in your invigorating scent, vitality I find."

6. Finally, as you add the orange essential oil, speak, "Orange, fruit of the sun, fill me with joy, let fatigue be undone."

7. Mix the ingredients thoroughly until the mixture is smooth and creamy. As you mix, visualize a bright,

yellow light filling the butter, charging it with energy and life.

8. Once your body butter is mixed, say, "This vitality butter is now complete, a balm for the body, both strong and sweet."

9. Transfer the body butter into your glass jar. Seal the jar and hold it between your hands, warming it with your energy and solidifying your intentions.

Sealing the Spell:

1. With the body butter in your storage jar, place it on a windowsill to charge in the sunlight, or under the moonlight to absorb the glow of the moon.

2. Finish the spell by affirming, "Charged by light, day or night, this butter brings health to light."

After the Spell:

1. When applying the body vitality butter, take a moment to massage it into your skin, focusing on areas that need extra care or energy.

2. As you use it, visualize its energy seeping into your body, revitalizing every cell and uplifting your spirits.

3. Store the butter in a cool place to maintain its texture and potency.

4. Use the butter daily as a reminder of your commitment to self-care and vitality.

5. Document how your body feels before and after application, and any changes in your overall energy levels, in your journal.

Your Body Vitality Butter is now ready to use, serving as a daily reaffirmation of your dedication to nurturing your body and spirit.

16. HEALING POPPET CHARM

Intent: To create a poppet as a focal point for healing energy, meant to represent the person to whom the healing is directed, whether it's yourself or someone else.

You Will Need:

- A small piece of white cloth to symbolize purity and healing
- Cotton or natural stuffing to fill your poppet
- Thread and needle for sewing the poppet
- Dried lavender for calm and restoration
- Dried rosemary for mental clarity and physical rejuvenation
- A small strip of paper and a pen to write down the name of the person or the specific healing intent
- A small amethyst crystal for its healing vibrations
- A blue ribbon to bind the poppet, representing healing energy

Preparation:

1. Set aside a quiet time and space where you can craft your poppet without interruptions.
2. Cleanse your space and all materials with your preferred method.

The Spell:

1. Cut two identical poppet shapes from the white cloth. As you cut, focus on the person you are creating the poppet for, envisioning them healthy and whole.

2. Sew the edges of the poppet together with the white thread, leaving a space to insert the stuffing. As you sew, chant, "Stitch by stitch, I sew to heal, with each thread, restoration I seal."

3. Write the name of the person or the healing intention on the strip of paper. Fold it and place it inside the poppet, affirming, "Your name I enclose, healing begins, through this poppet, the recovery wins."

4. Add the dried lavender and rosemary into the poppet along with the amethyst crystal. With each item, say, "Lavender, rosemary, and stone of amethyst, in this charm, your healing is manifest."

5. Fill the rest of the poppet with the stuffing, then sew it closed. Tie the blue ribbon around the poppet's neck or in a bow, stating, "Bound by blue, I seal this charm, a talisman of healing, no cause for alarm."

6. Hold the completed poppet in your hands, visualize a soft blue light surrounding it, and say, "Poppet of health, charm of ease, bring (name) comfort, let illness cease."

Sealing the Spell:

1. Place the poppet on your altar or in a special place where it can remain undisturbed, absorbing the healing intentions.

2. Light a candle nearby if you wish, letting its light represent the continuing presence of healing energy around the poppet.

3. When you feel the time is right, extinguish the candle, saying, "By light of fire, by warmth of heart, let health be whole, and pain depart."

After the Spell:

1. Whenever additional healing energy is needed, hold the poppet and repeat the visualization of blue light and the recitation of the incantation.

2. If the poppet is for someone else, you can give it to them with instructions to keep it in a safe place, or you can keep it and maintain the healing intent on their behalf.

3. Regularly check on the poppet, refreshing the herbs or the crystal's energy as needed.

4. Note any progress or signs of healing in yourself or the person the poppet is intended for, and record these observations in your journal.

This Healing Poppet Charm now stands as a beacon of comfort and recovery, a tangible representation of your healing intentions.

17. CUSTOM HEALING SIGIL

Intent: To design a personalized sigil that serves as a powerful symbol of health and healing for either physical or emotional wellbeing.

You Will Need:

- A piece of paper and a pen
- A quiet space to focus your intention
- A white candle for purity and healing energy
- Essential oils of your choice that correspond to healing (such as lavender, eucalyptus, or tea tree)
- A small cloth or parchment to create a talisman

Preparation:

1. Choose a time when you can work undisturbed, preferably when you feel calm and collected.
2. Cleanse your space and your materials, clearing away any energies that might interfere with your healing intentions.

The Spell:

1. Light the white candle, focusing on its flame as a beacon of healing and purity.

2. On the piece of paper, write a statement of intent that encapsulates the healing you seek, such as "I am whole, healthy, and free from pain."

3. Simplify this statement by removing vowels and repeating consonants, leaving you with a string of unique letters.

4. Begin to play with the shapes of these letters, overlapping them and combining them into a symbol that feels right to you. This is your healing sigil, a unique emblem of your health and wellbeing.

5. As you create your sigil, infuse it with your intention. Visualize the symbol glowing with a healing light, each line and curve imbued with the power to restore and revitalize.

6. Once satisfied with your sigil, anoint it with a drop of the essential oils, reinforcing its healing properties.

7. Transfer the sigil onto the cloth or parchment, recreating it with care and precision. As you do so, chant, "Mark of healing, symbol of rest, bring forth wellness, at my behest."

8. Hold the completed sigil in your hands, close your eyes, and take deep breaths. With each breath, imagine the sigil's energy growing stronger, radiating health and healing.

9. Conclude the creation of your sigil with the words, "This sigil now holds the power to heal, as I will it, so shall it be real."

Sealing the Spell:

1. Extinguish the candle, envisioning the smoke carrying your healing intentions out into the world.
2. Fold the cloth or parchment with the sigil on it, and keep it near you - under your pillow, in your wallet, or by your bedside.

After the Spell:

1. Whenever you need a boost of healing energy, hold the sigil in your hands and visualize its power activating and flowing through you.
2. If the sigil is for someone else, present it to them with instructions on how they can use it to aid their healing process.
3. Refresh the sigil's energy periodically by exposing it to moonlight or anointing it with essential oils.
4. Keep a healing journal to track your progress or the progress of the person you're helping to heal, noting any changes or improvements in wellbeing.

Your Custom Healing Sigil is now a potent tool in your journey toward health, a symbol of your commitment to nurturing your body and spirit.

18. PROTECTION AMULET

Intent: To create an amulet that serves as a guardian against negative influences, psychic attacks, and energetic harm.

You Will Need:
- A small pouch or a piece of black or deep purple cloth and ribbon
- A black tourmaline crystal for grounding and protection from negative energies
- A small sprig of rosemary or dried rosemary for mental clarity and spiritual protection
- A pinch of sea salt for purification and to ward off unwanted energies
- A piece of paper and a pen
- An essential oil blend with protective properties, such as frankincense for shielding and clove for banishing negativity
- A candle, preferably black or white, to represent the element of fire and its ability to ward off darkness

Preparation:
1. Choose a quiet and comfortable space where you won't be interrupted.

2. Cleanse your space, the candle, crystal, herbs, and cloth, using your preferred method, such as smoke from sage or palo santo, or sprinkling with saltwater.

The Spell:

1. Light the candle to begin your ritual, inviting the element of fire to provide strength and protection.

2. On the piece of paper, write down the protective intentions for your amulet, focusing on the specific types of protection you are seeking.

3. Fold the paper, concentrating on infusing the folds with your intent for security and safety.

4. Place the folded paper in the center of your cloth or open the pouch.

5. Add the black tourmaline crystal, stating, "Black tourmaline, stone of might, shield me with your protective light."

6. Sprinkle the pinch of sea salt over the paper and say, "Salt of the earth, cleanse and protect, keep me guarded from all neglect."

7. Lay the sprig or dried rosemary on top and chant, "Rosemary for remembrance, let not harm come my way, keep danger at bay."

8. Anoint the edges of the cloth or the opening of the pouch with the essential oil blend, invoking the

oil's protective properties with the words, "Oil of frankincense (and clove), create a shield, for my well-being shall not yield."

9. Pull the corners of the cloth together or draw the pouch's strings tight, and tie it securely while visualizing a barrier of protective light encasing the amulet.

10. Hold the amulet over the candle (carefully, so as not to burn it) and say, "By fire's might and earth's strength, I charge this amulet at length. Protect me from harm, this is my will, guarded and safe, by power instilled."

Sealing the Spell:

1. Blow out the candle, envisioning the smoke creating an impenetrable shield around you.

2. Keep the Protection Amulet with you, in your bag, pocket, or wear it as a necklace, ensuring you are within its protective aura at all times.

After the Spell:

1. Whenever you feel in need of extra protection, hold the amulet and visualize it activating, strengthening its protective barrier around you.

2. Regularly recharge the amulet by placing it in the sunlight or moonlight, and by reaffirming your protective intentions.

3. If the amulet is ever lost or damaged, take it as a sign that it has absorbed as much negativity as it can, and it is time to create a new one.

4. Document any feelings of safety, or any instances where you believe the amulet has protected you, in your journal.

This Protection Amulet now serves as your personal shield, charged with energies to keep you secure from harm.

19. BOUNDARY PROTECTION SALT

Intent: To create a sacred blend of salt that acts as a protective barrier for your home, safeguarding against negative energies and creating a boundary for psychic defense.

You Will Need:

- Coarse sea salt or Himalayan pink salt, known for their cleansing and protective qualities
- A mortar and pestle for combining and empowering your ingredients
- Dried rosemary for purification and protection
- Black peppercorns to ward off negative energies
- Essential oil of frankincense for its purifying and sanctifying properties
- A small jar or container to house the salt
- A piece of parchment or paper
- A pen for writing protective symbols or intentions

Preparation:

1. Begin by finding a peaceful time and space where you can work uninterrupted.

2. Cleanse your working area, the mortar and pestle, and all of your ingredients using your preferred method, like smudging with sage or palo santo.

The Spell:

1. Light a candle if you wish to incorporate the element of fire into your ritual for extra cleansing and protective energy.

2. In the mortar and pestle, start by grinding the dried rosemary to release its cleansing properties, focusing on your intent to purify and protect your space. As you grind, chant, "Rosemary for protection, ward off the unwanted, guard my direction."

3. Add the black peppercorns to the mortar. As you grind them with the rosemary, visualize creating a barrier impervious to negative energies. Say, "Peppercorns so black, repel negativity back."

4. Mix in a generous amount of sea salt, pouring your intentions of safety and purity into the blend, with words like, "Salt of the earth, form a shield, by this mixture, my safety's sealed."

5. Place a few drops of frankincense oil into the mix, and as the aroma rises, feel it sanctifying your salt blend. Recite, "Frankincense holy, bless this salt, in your strength, I shall not fault."

6. Pour the mixture into your chosen jar or container. If you have specific protective symbols or words of power, write them on the parchment paper, fold it, and place it beneath or within the jar. As you do this, say, "Symbols of power, signs of might, secure my home, both day and night."

7. Seal the jar tightly, and if you used a candle, drip a little wax onto the lid as a seal. Affirm with, "This seal is set, the charm is cast, around this home, protection lasts."

Sealing the Spell:

1. Place the jar in a central location of your home or near the entryway. Alternatively, sprinkle some of the salt across thresholds, windowsills, or around the property's boundary, wherever you feel a protective barrier is needed.

2. As you place or sprinkle the salt, envision a glowing barrier forming, encapsulating your home in a protective sphere. Say, "By this salt, a boundary made, within, without, let not fade."

After the Spell: Whenever you feel the need, reinforce the salt barriers, especially after cleaning, after guests leave, or at the change of seasons.

1. Take note of the sense of peace and security within your space, and record any shifts or changes in your environment or your feelings.

2. Maintain the potency of the Boundary Protection Salt by re-empowering it at regular intervals, such as during the full moon or after a significant life event.

The Boundary Protection Salt is now a bastion of your personal space, a sacred guard against the unseen, ensuring peace and security within your sanctified walls.

20. HOME PROTECTION WASH

Intent: To infuse your home with protective energies, cleanse away negativity, and create a barrier against unwanted influences.

You Will Need:

- Warm water as a base for your wash
- Sea salt or Himalayan pink salt for grounding and protection
- Rosemary essential oil for mental clarity and purification
- Fresh or dried rosemary for added protection
- White vinegar for cleansing negative energies
- A fresh lemon, sliced, for purification and to invite positive energy
- A clean bucket or container for preparing the wash

Preparation:

1. Tidy up your home, as a clean space is more receptive to protective energies.
2. Open all windows and doors to allow fresh air to carry away any stagnant energy.

3. Assemble all your ingredients and place them within easy reach.

The Spell:

1. Fill the bucket or container with warm water, envisioning it as a glowing vessel of protective light.

2. Stir in the sea salt, visualizing each grain dissolving negativity and reinforcing your home's protective shield.

3. Add several drops of rosemary essential oil while chanting, "Essence of rosemary, guard my home, preserve the peace within its dome."

4. Submerge the sprig of rosemary or sprinkle in the dried rosemary as you say, "Rosemary, herb of protection, lend strength and direction."

5. Pour in the white vinegar, affirming its purifying power with the words, "Vinegar strong, cleanse and protect, let only joy and peace connect."

6. Squeeze the lemon slices into the wash, or drop them in whole, saying, "Lemon bright, cleanse and purify, fill this space with energy high."

Sealing the Spell:

1. Starting at your front door, use the wash to cleanse the threshold, moving clockwise through your home

and gently sprinkling or wiping surfaces with the wash.

2. With each application, visualize a bright barrier forming, sealing each room with protective light.

3. Conclude at the front door, affirming, "This home is now a fortress strong; within its walls, we belong."

After the Spell:

1. Dispose of the leftover wash outside, returning it to the earth, and close all windows and doors, finalizing the protective boundary.

2. Light a candle or incense as a final act of purification and to fill the space with a comforting scent.

3. Rest in the tranquility of your newly cleansed and protected home, taking comfort in the peace you've cultivated.

4. Regularly refresh the protective energies with this wash, maintaining the intention of a secure and harmonious home.

This Home Protection Wash is now an integral part of your domestic well-being, enveloping your living space in layers of protective energy and serenity.

21. ABUNDANCE MINT TEA

Intent: To attract abundance and prosperity into your life while enjoying a refreshing and invigorating tea ritual.

You Will Need:

- Fresh mint leaves or mint tea for attracting financial success
- A green tea bag as a base for growth and prosperity
- A slice of ginger or a pinch of powdered ginger for adding energy and speed to your intentions
- A teaspoon of honey for sweet success and enjoyment
- A lemon slice for clarity and to invite positive opportunities
- A cup or teapot for brewing the tea
- Boiling water

Preparation:

1. Gather all your ingredients and place them on your kitchen counter or table, where you will prepare the tea.
2. Cleanse your space with the intention of making it receptive to abundance.

The Spell:

1. Begin by boiling water, visualizing it as the bubbling, energetic foundation for your spell.

2. Place the mint leaves or tea bag into your cup or teapot, saying, "Mint, herb of wealth, bring prosperity with your refreshing health."

3. Add the green tea bag, affirming, "Green tea, plant of growth, let my finances expand, not be loath."

4. Place the slice of ginger into the mix, or sprinkle the powdered ginger, while chanting, "Ginger root, spice of fire, to abundant life I aspire."

5. Pour the boiling water over these ingredients, watching it blend and infuse with the herbs and spices, while stating, "Water hot and herbs combine, attract abundance that's truly mine."

6. Stir in the honey, enjoying the sweet aroma, and say, "Honey gold, sweet and rich, let prosperity come without a hitch."

7. Squeeze the lemon slice into the tea, adding brightness and zing, and declare, "Lemon clear, bring opportunities here."

Sealing the Spell:

1. Allow the tea to steep, infusing your drink with your intentions of abundance and success.

2. Once the tea is ready, hold the cup in both hands, feeling the warmth, and imagine it filling you with a golden light of prosperity.

3. Take a sip, and as you do, say, "With each sip, I seal this spell, abundance flows, all is well."

After the Spell:

1. Drink the tea mindfully, savoring each sip, and visualize yourself achieving the prosperity and success you desire.

2. Dispose of the tea leaves or bag by returning them to the earth, thanking them for their energy and essence.

3. Carry forward this sense of abundance throughout your day, looking for opportunities to grow and prosper.

4. Keep a journal to note any positive changes in your financial situation or any new opportunities that come your way.

With this Abundance Mint Tea ritual complete, you've set the wheels of prosperity in motion, ready to enjoy the plentiful harvest that life has to offer.

22. CLARITY TEA SPELL

Intent: To brew a tea that will clear the mind, enhance insight, and improve focus on personal goals and decisions.

You Will Need:

- A clear quartz crystal for mental clarity
- Chamomile tea for relaxation and mental calm
- Peppermint leaves or peppermint tea for heightened awareness and energy
- A slice of lemon for purification and to promote clear thinking
- A teaspoon of honey for sweetness and to reinforce the positive intentions
- A kettle or pot for boiling water
- A mug or cup for serving the tea

Preparation:

1. Place the clear quartz near your tea brewing area to charge the space with its clarifying energy.
2. Ensure your kitchen or tea-making space is tidy, promoting a clear environment for a clear mind.

The Spell:

1. Heat the water in your kettle or pot until it reaches a rolling boil, symbolizing the activation of energy and intention.

2. As you place the chamomile tea into your cup, speak the words, "Chamomile, herb of peace, release my mind from its fleece."

3. Add the peppermint leaves or tea, stating, "Peppermint, brisk and bright, grant me clarity, grant me insight."

4. Pour the hot water over the tea, envisioning the steam as the lifting of fog, revealing the sharpness of clear thought.

5. Stir the tea with a spoon, clockwise, saying, "As I stir this brew, let clarity come through."

6. Squeeze the lemon slice into the tea, watching as its essence disperses, and declare, "Lemon cleanse, make my thoughts pure, in my decisions, let me be sure."

7. Sweeten the tea with honey, affirming, "With this honey, I sweeten my day, let clarity shine in every way."

Sealing the Spell:

1. Let the tea steep until it's strong and aromatic, indicating that your intentions are well-infused.

2. Hold the cup, feeling its warmth, and visualize a light of clarity enveloping your mind, bringing sharpness, focus, and understanding.

3. Before taking the first sip, affirm with conviction, "I drink this tea, and with it see, the path ahead clear for me."

After the Spell:

1. Sip the tea slowly, savoring each mouthful, and focus on the issues or questions that require clarity.

2. Rinse the clear quartz under running water and carry it with you or place it in a space where you make decisions, as a reminder of your intent.

3. Reflect on the clarity gained in your tea ritual, and write down any insights or ideas in your journal.

4. Continue to seek out moments of calm and clarity, reinforcing the spell's power in your daily life.

This Clarity Tea Spell is a simple yet powerful way to align your thoughts and intentions, opening the door to a more focused and insightful mindset.

23. GOOD LUCK SPELL

Intent: To enhance your fortunes and open pathways for luck to flow into your life, creating opportunities for positive outcomes and success.

You Will Need:

- A green candle to symbolize luck and prosperity
- Basil leaves for attracting good fortune
- Cinnamon for quick success and action
- Nutmeg to bring good luck
- A small piece of jade or aventurine, stones associated with luck
- An orange, for its association with good luck and abundance
- A piece of paper and a pen to write down where you need luck

Preparation:

1. Arrange a quiet and comfortable space for the spell where you can focus without interruptions.
2. Clean the area physically and spiritually, allowing for a fresh energy conducive to luck.

The Spell:

1. Light the green candle, envisioning its flame as a beacon for luck, illuminating opportunities and fortunate circumstances.

2. Write down the areas in your life where you seek luck's favor. Fold the paper, concentrating on your wishes as you do so.

3. Sprinkle basil leaves around the candle, affirming, "Basil, herb of luck, bring fortune my way, and never amuck."

4. Dust cinnamon over the basil, saying, "Cinnamon spice, bring success fast, may good fortune come and last."

5. Grate a bit of nutmeg into the mix, chanting, "Nutmeg warm, enhance my charm, and bring good luck into my arm."

6. Place the piece of jade or aventurine near the base of the candle to charge with your intentions, stating, "Stone of luck, with you near, I call good fortune to appear."

7. Peel the orange, releasing its citrus scent, and say, "Orange bright, bring luck's delight, may my days be sunny and light."

Sealing the Spell:

1. Sit quietly with the candle, watching its flame dance. Visualize scenarios unfolding with the luck you have called upon manifesting in real and tangible ways.

2. Once the candle has burned down safely, or after a time you feel appropriate, blow it out, sending your intentions out into the universe, and say, "My wishes are clear, my intentions are cast, good luck is mine, and fortune amassed."

After the Spell:

1. Carry the jade or aventurine stone with you, especially in situations where you feel you need a bit of extra luck.

2. Eat the orange as a physical acceptance of the luck coming your way.

3. Dispose of the basil, cinnamon, and nutmeg respectfully, returning them to the earth if possible.

4. Keep the folded piece of paper in a safe place, like your wallet or purse, as a reminder of the luck you have summoned.

5. Observe the changes in your life, no matter how small, and make note of any "lucky" happenings in your journal.

This Good Luck Spell sets the stage for serendipity, paving the way for prosperity and the happy twists of fate that bring joy and success into your life.

24. UNDERSTANDING SPELL

Intent: To open your mind and heart to deeper comprehension and empathy, fostering better communication and relationships with others.

You Will Need:

- A blue candle for calm communication and understanding
- Lavender oil for clarity and peace
- Sodalite or lapis lazuli, stones known for enhancing understanding and insight
- Sage leaves or sage incense for wisdom and cleansing
- A small bowl of water to represent emotional clarity
- A piece of paper and a pen to write down your intention or a question you seek to understand

Preparation:

1. Find a quiet place where you can focus on the spell without distractions.
2. Clean your space, ideally using sage smoke, to purify the area and your mind.

The Spell:

1. Light the blue candle, and as you focus on its flame, invite tranquility and clear communication.

2. Write down your intention or the specific situation you wish to understand better on the piece of paper.

3. Anoint the candle with a drop of lavender oil while you focus on your desire for clarity and insight.

4. Place the sodalite or lapis lazuli stone near the candle to absorb and magnify the energies of understanding.

5. Pass the sage leaves or burn the sage incense around the candle, saying, "Sage so wise, sage so clear, rid confusion, bring understanding near."

6. Fold the paper and place it under the bowl of water, envisioning the water's purity soaking through to your written words, signifying clear perception.

7. Gaze into the bowl of water, and take a moment to open your mind to any new insights or perspectives that may come to you.

Sealing the Spell:

1. Allow the candle to burn down safely while you meditate on the flame, absorbing the calmness and clarity it represents.

2. Once the candle has burned sufficiently, extinguish it, affirming, "By light of blue, my mind is open, understanding granted, empathy woken."

3. Take out the piece of paper, dry it if necessary, and keep it in a place where you study or meditate.

After the Spell:

1. Carry the sodalite or lapis lazuli with you when you engage in discussions or seek to learn, as a reminder to listen and understand deeply.

2. Reflect on any new understandings that arise after performing the spell, and be open to the gentle guidance of empathy in your interactions.

3. Dispose of the sage respectfully, and consider ending your ritual with a few deep, cleansing breaths to internalize the spell's intention.

4. Note any improvements in your ability to understand or connect with others in your journal, acknowledging the spell's influence on your growth.

This Understanding Spell is a gentle yet powerful way to enhance your receptive and interpretive powers, guiding you towards greater clarity and connection in your interactions.

25. HALTING ILL INTENTIONS SPELL

Intent: To protect oneself from the negative intentions or harmful energies directed by others, creating a shield that neutralizes malice and ill will.

You Will Need:

- A black candle for absorbing negativity
- A piece of obsidian or black tourmaline for grounding and protection
- Salt for purification and protection
- A clove of garlic or garlic skin for banishment
- A small mirror or reflective surface to deflect ill intentions
- A bay leaf to represent victory over negativity
- A small bowl of water to cleanse and dissipate negative energy

Preparation:

1. Set up a quiet space where you will not be disturbed, preferably in a place where you feel most secure.
2. Clean your area, the candle, and the reflective surface using smoke from sage or incense to ensure they are free of previous energies.

The Spell:

1. Light the black candle, and as you do, visualize it creating a dark sphere around you that absorbs and neutralizes negativity.

2. Hold the piece of obsidian or black tourmaline, and state your intent to be protected. Place it before the candle.

3. Surround the base of the candle with a circle of salt, affirming, "Salt that purifies, protect me now, encircle me with your sacred vow."

4. If using a clove of garlic, break it to release its scent, or if using garlic skin, tear it to symbolize the breaking of negative intentions. Say, "Garlic that wards, keep harm at bay, banish ill will, far away."

5. Place the mirror before you, reflective side outwards, and speak, "Mirror bright, reflect and fend, send all harm back to its sender's end."

6. Lay the bay leaf over the mirror and say, "Bay for triumph, bay for might, ensure my victory in this fight."

7. Dip your fingers in the bowl of water, flicking droplets around your space while visualizing each drop cleansing the air of malice and ill intent.

Sealing the Spell:

1. Sit quietly, visualizing the candle's flame expanding to reinforce the protective energies around you.

2. Affirm with confidence, "No ill or harm comes to me, protected I am, so mote it be."

3. Let the candle burn down safely, or extinguish it knowing that your intent has been set and your protection is in place.

After the Spell:

1. Keep the obsidian or black tourmaline with you, especially in situations where you feel vulnerable to negativity.

2. Dispose of the garlic outside, away from your home, to carry away any remnants of ill will.

3. Clean the mirror and keep it in a place where it can continue to deflect negativity, or carry it with you as a shield.

4. Write down the details of the spell and any specific feelings or experiences associated with it in your journal.

5. Refresh this spell as needed, especially if you feel a surge of negative intentions coming your way.

With the Halting Ill Intentions Spell, you have set a powerful energetic barrier, affirming your right to a peaceful and protected existence free from the undue influence of others' negative wishes.

26. REPAIRING A RIFT SPELL

Intent: To mend misunderstandings and heal emotional wounds that have caused a separation or conflict, fostering forgiveness and reconciliation.

You Will Need:

- A blue candle for healing and peace
- A photograph or personal item representing the relationship in need of repair
- A small bowl of water to symbolize emotional healing
- A pinch of salt to purify intentions and absorb negativity
- Rose quartz to promote unconditional love and harmony
- Basil for fostering understanding and empathy
- Honey to sweeten interactions and soften hearts
- Two pieces of string or thread to symbolize the connection between individuals

Preparation:

1. Find a quiet space where you can focus on the intention of the spell without disturbances.

2. Cleanse your environment and all items you'll be using to ensure they carry only positive energy.

The Spell:

1. Light the blue candle, and as you do, set your intention for healing and reconciliation.

2. Place the photograph or personal item in front of the candle, letting it be touched by the warm, healing light.

3. Sprinkle the salt into the bowl of water, stating, "Salt cleanse away the hurt and pain, let only love and forgiveness remain."

4. Place the rose quartz in the bowl, visualizing it emitting a soothing, loving energy, and say, "Rose quartz, stone of heart, heal this rift, bring a fresh start."

5. Add a drop of honey to the water, and as it diffuses, chant, "Sweeten our thoughts, sweeten our speech, let understanding each of us reach."

6. Hold one piece of string in each hand, representing both sides of the rift. Slowly tie them together while saying, "What was parted, now mend, with goodwill and love, let the rift end."

Sealing the Spell:

1. Visualize the rift healing as the strings are tied together, forming a strong, reconnected bond.
2. Say, "By knot and candle, by water and stone, let the bridge be built, let love be shown."
3. Allow the candle to burn down while the strings, photograph, and bowl remain in place, solidifying the intent of the spell.

After the Spell:

1. Keep the tied strings and rose quartz on or near the photograph or personal item, symbolizing ongoing healing and connection.
2. Dispose of the water by pouring it onto the earth, signifying the release of any residual negativity and the grounding of positive intentions.
3. Reflect on the actions you can take in the physical world to complement the spell, like reaching out or extending a gesture of peace.
4. Note in your journal the date of the spell and any subsequent developments in the relationship.

With the Repairing a Rift Spell cast, you've set the foundation for mending and reconciliation, opening the way for dialogue, understanding, and a renewed bond.

27. STRENGTHENING FRIENDSHIPS SPELL

Intent: To reinforce the bonds of friendship, ensuring mutual support, understanding, and enduring connection.

You Will Need:

- A pink candle for affection and friendship
- Two rose quartz crystals to represent each friend in the bond
- Chamomile flowers for relaxation and harmony
- Cinnamon sticks for warmth and to spice up the friendship
- A small charm or token that symbolizes your friendship
- Lavender oil for calm communication and trust
- A ribbon to symbolize the tying together of friendship

Preparation:

1. Choose a time when you and your friend are both at ease, perhaps even performing the spell together for added intention.
2. Cleanse the area where you will perform the spell, encouraging a positive and welcoming space.

The Spell:

1. Light the pink candle, allowing its light to cast a warm glow over your spell-working area.

2. Hold the rose quartz crystals in your hands, warming them with your energy and intention for a strong, healthy friendship.

3. Place the chamomile flowers around the base of the candle, saying, "Chamomile, herb of peace, nurture the roots of our friendship lease."

4. Lay the cinnamon sticks in front of the candle and speak, "Cinnamon, spice of fire, keep our friendship filled with desire for fun and growth."

5. Anoint the charm or token with lavender oil, and say, "Lavender for trust and clear expression, bless this charm, protect our connection."

6. Place the anointed charm between the rose quartz crystals, and tie them together gently with the ribbon, affirming, "This ribbon binds our friendship tight, through days of joy and darkest nights."

Sealing the Spell:

1. Focus on the flame of the pink candle, visualizing it glowing brighter, representing the growing strength and warmth of your friendship.

2. As the candle burns, recite, "This friendship is true, this friendship is bright, may it grow stronger both day and night."

3. Allow the candle to burn down safely while the crystals and charm remain close to it, absorbing the energies of your spell.

After the Spell:

1. Keep the tied crystals and charm in a special place, such as your bedroom or another area where you spend a lot of time, to keep the energy of the spell active.

2. Give one of the rose quartz crystals to your friend as a token of the spell and to maintain the connection.

3. Sprinkle the chamomile flowers outside, releasing any remaining energies of the spell into the universe.

4. Reflect on your actions and words when with your friend, ensuring they align with the intentions of the spell.

5. Note any positive changes or moments that reflect the strength of your friendship in your journal.

The Strengthening Friendships Spell is designed to fortify the bonds you share, bringing joy, understanding, and lasting camaraderie to both you and your friend.

28. ARGUMENT CLEARING SPELL

Intent: To dissipate the negative energy from an argument and to open the channels for clear, compassionate communication.

You Will Need:

- A white candle for peace and new beginnings
- Clear quartz crystal to amplify clarity and understanding
- A bowl of water to symbolize emotional clarity and to wash away conflict
- Basil leaves for harmony and to foster goodwill
- A piece of paper to write down points of contention
- A blue ribbon to represent healing and calm communication

Preparation:

1. Find a quiet moment when you can focus your energies without interruption.
2. Tidy the space where you will cast the spell, creating a peaceful environment.

The Spell:

1. Light the white candle and take a moment to watch the flame, focusing on its purity and steadiness.

2. Hold the clear quartz crystal in your hand, envisioning it filling with the light of the candle, and set the intention for it to bring clarity and calm to the situation.

3. Write the issues or negative feelings from the argument on the piece of paper, pouring your wish for resolution into each word.

4. Place the basil leaves in the bowl of water, and as they soak, imagine them diffusing soothing energy to heal any discord.

5. Submerge the piece of paper in the water, watching as the ink disperses, symbolizing the dissolving of the argument.

6. Wrap the blue ribbon around the bowl, saying, "With this ribbon, I bind the spell, calm and peace now will dwell."

Sealing the Spell:

1. Sit quietly with the bowl, focusing on the water's surface, and affirm, "Clear and calm, the waters run, let the discord now be done."

2. Let the candle burn down safely, allowing the energies of peace and clarity to fill the space.

3. When the candle has burned out, remove the paper and basil from the water, and dispose of them outside, returning the issues to the earth.

After the Spell:

1. Keep the clear quartz nearby when you communicate next with the person involved in the argument, to encourage positive dialogue.

2. Reflect on the argument and your role in it, considering ways to approach future disagreements with calm and clarity.

3. Note any changes in the atmosphere or in the dynamics of the relationship, acknowledging the spell's influence on your interactions.

With the Argument Clearing Spell, you have taken proactive steps to remove negative vibrations from an argument, paving the way for constructive communication and a return to mutual understanding.

29. SEVEN-DAY HEALTH CANDLE SPELL

Intent: To promote ongoing health and well-being over the course of a week, focusing on physical, mental, and spiritual vitality.

You Will Need:

- A large white candle that can burn for seven days, for overall health and purification
- A marker to inscribe the candle with symbols or words of health
- Essential oils associated with healing such as eucalyptus, tea tree, or lavender
- Seven small pieces of paper to write daily affirmations of health
- A heatproof dish or candle holder
- Fresh herbs such as rosemary for mental clarity, mint for digestive health, and sage for immunity

Preparation:

1. Select a safe space where the candle can burn undisturbed and is not a fire hazard.
2. Ensure the area is clean and serene, conducive to healing energies.

The Spell:

1. Begin by inscribing the candle with symbols or words that you associate with health and healing.

2. Anoint the candle with a few drops of the chosen essential oil(s), spreading them with your fingers and focusing on imbuing the candle with healing properties.

3. Place the candle in its holder or dish, making sure it's secure.

4. Write your health affirmations on the small pieces of paper—one for each day of the coming week.

5. Place the first affirmation under the candle holder or dish.

6. Surround the base of the candle with the fresh herbs, inviting their natural healing properties to join your spell.

The Spell (Day 1):

1. Light the candle, focusing on igniting the flame of health within you.

2. Recite the affirmation for the day, allowing its words to resonate with your being.

3. Spend a few minutes in meditation, visualizing yourself or the intended recipient of the spell as vibrant and healthy.

Continuation (Days 2-7): Each day, light the candle at approximately the same time. Replace the affirmation paper with the new day's affirmation, and recite it aloud. Reinforce your visualization of robust health and spend some time in quiet reflection or meditation on the day's specific health focus.

Sealing the Spell:

1. On the seventh day, after reciting the final affirmation, allow the candle to continue burning until it goes out on its own, signifying the completion of your week-long health focus.

2. Gather the pieces of paper with the affirmations and either bury them, burn them safely, or keep them somewhere meaningful as a reminder of your commitment to health.

After the Spell:

1. Reflect on any changes in your health throughout the week, acknowledging improvements and feelings of increased vitality.

2. Dispose of the herb remnants in a respectful way, returning them to nature if possible.

3. Consider making this seven-day health focus a regular practice, perhaps once a month or at the change of seasons, to maintain and enhance your well-being.

This Seven-Day Health Candle Spell acts as a sustained effort to boost your health and encourage continuous mindfulness regarding your well-being.

30. FORGIVENESS TAROT RITUAL

Intent: To use the symbolic power of the tarot to help release grudges and to foster forgiveness, whether it's forgiving yourself or others.

You Will Need:

- A tarot deck, with the cards Strength, Judgment, and The Star specifically identified
- A white candle for purity of intention and new beginnings
- A small bowl of water as a symbol of emotional purification
- Rose quartz to promote forgiveness and compassion
- Sage, palo santo, or incense for cleansing your space
- A piece of paper and pen to write down what or who you are forgiving

Preparation:

1. Select a quiet and calm space where you can perform the ritual without being disturbed.
2. Cleanse the area with the sage, palo santo, or incense, allowing the smoke to clear away any negative energy.

The Ritual:

1. Light the white candle, setting the intention for clarity and cleansing.

2. Place the Strength card before you, focusing on the card's message of inner strength and courage to forgive.

3. Write down the name or situation you wish to forgive on the piece of paper. Fold it and place it under the bowl of water.

4. Lay the rose quartz next to the bowl, asking it to fill your heart with unconditional love and the grace to forgive.

5. Set the Judgment card next to the rose quartz, contemplating its theme of release and renewal.

6. Reflect on the feelings that come up, and when you feel ready, place the Star card on top of the other two cards, focusing on its message of hope and healing.

7. Say aloud, "With strength, I face my pain, with judgment, I release it, and with the Star, I heal and forgive."

Sealing the Ritual:

1. Spend a few moments meditating on the feeling of release and the lightness that comes with forgiveness.

2. When you're ready, blow out the candle, visualizing the dissipating smoke as the remnants of your grudge or pain leaving you.

3. Remove the piece of paper from under the bowl, and if possible, burn it safely to symbolize the final release of those feelings.

After the Ritual:

1. Keep the rose quartz with you, or place it in an area where you'll see it often as a reminder to maintain a forgiving and loving heart.

2. Dispose of the ashes from the burned paper respectfully, perhaps by scattering them outside.

3. Reflect on the experience in your journal, noting any insights or feelings that arose during the ritual.

4. Return to the Star card periodically as a meditation focus, reaffirming your commitment to healing and moving forward.

This Forgiveness Tarot Ritual is a symbolic journey through the process of forgiveness, harnessing the archetypal wisdom of the tarot to guide you towards letting go of old wounds and embracing a renewed sense of peace.

31. TRAVEL BLESSING CHARM

Intent: To craft a charm that ensures safety and good experiences during travel, protecting the bearer from misfortunes and guiding them to positive encounters.

You Will Need:

- A small pouch or a piece of cloth and ribbon to create a charm bag
- Comfrey for safe travel
- A St. Christopher medal, the patron saint of travelers, for protection
- A small piece of turquoise or aquamarine, stones known for their protective travel associations
- Lavender for calmness during travel
- A piece of paper and pen to write down your travel intentions and destinations
- Mint leaves for alertness and a refreshing energy while traveling

Preparation:

1. Gather your materials in a quiet space where you can concentrate on the charm without interruption.

2. Clean the space and materials with the smoke of sage or by visualizing a bright light purifying them.

The Spell:

1. Hold the comfrey in your hand and say, "Comfrey for safety, keep harm at bay, protect me as I travel each day."

2. Attach the St. Christopher medal to the pouch or place it in the center of the cloth, and affirm, "St. Christopher by my side, be my guide on this ride."

3. Place the turquoise or aquamarine in the pouch or on the cloth, and state, "Stone of seas, guard my way, in the air, on roads, or where I stay."

4. Add the lavender to the charm, saying, "Lavender for peace, soothe my path, make my journey free from wrath."

5. Write your travel intentions and destinations on the piece of paper, fold it tightly, and put it in the pouch or on the cloth, and chant, "Intentions set, the way is clear, bring me to my destinations near and dear."

6. Lastly, place the mint leaves in the pouch, and as you do so, say, "Mint for energy, keep me awake, to all the joys travel can make."

Sealing the Spell:

1. Tie up the pouch or gather the corners of the cloth
    and tie it with the ribbon, sealing all the items inside
    while saying, "This travel blessing charm is now
    complete, to ensure my travels are safe and sweet."

2. Hold the charm in both hands, close your eyes, and
    visualize yourself being surrounded by a protective
    light throughout your travels.

After the Spell:

1. Keep the travel blessing charm with you at all times
    during your travels— in your luggage, carry-on, or
    pocket.

2. Whenever you feel anxious or unsure while traveling,
    hold the charm to remind you of the protective
    energies it contains.

3. After your travels, open the charm and give thanks
    to each item for its protection and support. Cleanse
    the items and save them for your next journey.

4. Record any moments from your travels where
    you felt the charm's protection or guidance was
    particularly evident.

This Travel Blessing Charm serves as your magical
companion on your journeys, imbuing them with protection,
safety, and the promise of memorable experiences.

32. SUCCESS SIGIL

Intent: To create a personal symbol that attracts success and achievement in your endeavors.

You Will Need:

- A piece of paper and a pen
- A green candle for prosperity and success
- Basil leaves, associated with success and wealth
- Cinnamon, for quick and positive results
- An orange, for opportunities and good fortune
- A small pouch or cloth to carry the sigil

Preparation:

1. Choose a time when you feel positive and focused on your goals.
2. Cleanse your space to remove any distractions or negative energies.

The Spell:

1. Begin by lighting the green candle, visualizing its flame igniting the fire of success within you.
2. Write the word "SUCCESS" on the piece of paper. Concentrate on what success means to you and your specific goals.

3. Draw from the letters in "SUCCESS" to create your sigil. This can be an abstract design that represents your aspirations for achievement.

4. Place the basil leaves and cinnamon around the candle, and say, "Basil and cinnamon, herbs of might, bring success to my sight."

5. Take the orange and hold it for a moment, focusing on the zestful energy it represents. Then, place it next to your sigil, affirming, "Orange of fortune, round and true, roll success to me anew."

6. Once the sigil is created, pass it through the candle's flame (carefully) and the smoke of the herbs, imbuing it with the energies of growth and prosperity.

Sealing the Spell:

1. Fold the paper with the sigil written on it and place it inside the small pouch or cloth.

2. Tie the pouch closed or the cloth with a string, and while doing so, affirm, "With this sigil now enclosed, let the doors to success be opened and unopposed."

3. Extinguish the candle, knowing that the energy you've raised is now working towards manifesting your success.

After the Spell:

1. Carry the sigil with you, especially when heading towards situations where you need success—interviews, meetings, presentations.

2. Regularly hold the pouch and visualize your success, reinforcing the intention and energy of the sigil.

3. Upon achieving your goals, open the pouch, thank the sigil for its guidance, and safely burn the paper to release its energy.

4. Keep the herbs and orange peel in a place where you make decisions or work on your projects, to keep the scent and presence of success around you.

5. Document your progress towards your goals and the moments of success you encounter, recognizing the power of your sigil.

With the Success Sigil, you harness the power of your intention and the universe's energy to create a pathway for achievement and prosperity.

33. WEAVING SUCCESS SPELL

Intent: To metaphorically weave your path with threads of success, ensuring that your endeavors are met with positive outcomes.

You Will Need:
- A yellow candle for success and optimism
- Three different colored threads or yarns representing aspects of success (e.g., green for growth, blue for wisdom, gold for prosperity)
- A small loom or a makeshift frame for weaving
- Bay leaves for glory and triumph
- A clear quartz crystal to amplify your intentions
- A piece of paper and a pen to write down your goals

Preparation:
1. Set up your workspace with the loom or frame, ensuring it's clean and free of clutter.
2. Ground yourself and focus on the success you want to achieve, visualizing each goal clearly.

The Spell:
1. Light the yellow candle, contemplating the flame's power to manifest success.

2. Write your goals on the piece of paper. Place it beneath the loom or frame as a foundation for your spell.

3. Begin weaving with your threads, focusing on a specific aspect of success with each color. As you weave, chant, "Threads of success, weave your way, through the tapestry of my days."

4. Intertwine the bay leaves into your weave, saying, "Bay leaves for victory, weave into my destiny."

5. Place the clear quartz crystal near the loom, charging the entire setup with success-enhancing energy, and declare, "Quartz crystal clear, amplify my intentions here."

6. Continue weaving until you feel your work is complete, visualizing your goals coming to fruition with each thread.

Sealing the Spell:

1. Once your weave is complete, tie off the ends while affirming, "With this knot, I seal my fate, success is mine, for this I state."

2. Snuff out the candle, acknowledging the work done and the success that awaits.

3. Keep the woven piece in your workspace or another area where you engage in your projects or planning.

After the Spell:

1. Hold the clear quartz crystal whenever you need clarity or a boost of intention towards your goals.

2. Reflect on the weave as a physical representation of your path to success, and keep it in a place that inspires you to continue working towards your goals.

3. Periodically revisit the piece of paper with your goals written on it to track your progress and remind yourself of the intentions set during the spell.

4. As you achieve each goal, you may choose to remove a bay leaf or a thread from the weave, acknowledging the success and releasing that energy back into the universe.

The Weaving Success Spell is a creative and tangible way to draw the threads of fate towards a pattern of success, with each strand representing a stepping stone on the journey to achieving your ambitions.

34. ABUNDANCE BALM

Intent: To create a soothing balm that attracts abundance and prosperity, while also providing a pleasant, calming effect when applied.

You Will Need:

- A base balm or carrier oil like almond oil or coconut oil, which will be infused with herbs and crystals
- Beeswax, to give the balm consistency and to symbolize industry and effort leading to reward
- Basil leaves, known for attracting financial success and abundance
- Cinnamon, to draw quick and positive results in financial matters
- A small citrine crystal, as it is associated with wealth and abundance
- Essential oil of bergamot for prosperity and uplifting energy
- A clean tin, jar, or container to store your abundance balm
- A double boiler for melting and mixing your balm ingredients

Preparation:

1. Cleanse your workspace, all tools, and ingredients energetically to ensure they are ready to receive and hold your intention of abundance.

2. Assemble your tools and ingredients, laying them out neatly in the order you will use them.

The Spell:

1. Begin by melting the beeswax in the double boiler. As it melts, concentrate on the abundance you wish to attract.

2. Slowly add the carrier oil to the melted beeswax, stirring continuously and envisioning your balm filling with golden light.

3. Crush the basil leaves, releasing their scent and essence, and sprinkle them into the mixture, saying, "Basil herb of wealth, infuse this balm with abundant health."

4. Sprinkle cinnamon into the balm, and as you do, chant, "Cinnamon spice of prosperous flame, bring success to my name."

5. Hold the citrine crystal in your hand, warming it with your energy, and then place it atop the mixture (ensure it's clean and heatproof) as you say, "Citrine

stone of fortune bright, bless this balm with your light."

6. Add a few drops of bergamot essential oil, its citrus scent enhancing the mix, and state, "Bergamot for good fortune's call, ensure abundance comes to all."

Sealing the Spell:

1. Pour the mixture into your chosen container, carefully removing the citrine crystal (which can be carried separately as a talisman).

2. As the balm begins to solidify, visualize your life flourishing with abundance, from your finances to your personal happiness.

3. Once the balm has set, seal the container with the lid and say, "With this balm, I seal my fate, and open my life to abundance great."

After the Spell:

1. Apply the balm to your pulse points when you wish to remind yourself of your worth and to attract prosperity.

2. Keep the citrine crystal near your workspace or wallet as a continuous attractor of wealth.

3. Dispose of the basil leaves and cinnamon remnants respectfully, returning them to the earth.

4. Note any changes in your financial situation or feelings of abundance in your journal, acknowledging the role of your balm.

With the Abundance Balm prepared, you now have a physical manifestation of your intent to draw prosperity into your life, ready to be used as a daily reminder of the richness of the world.

35. NEW MOON FRIENDSHIP SPELL

Intent: To sow the seeds for new friendships or to nurture and deepen existing ones, taking advantage of the new moon's energy for beginnings and growth.

You Will Need:

- A small new moon ritual setup with a representation of the moon (could be a drawing, a photo, or a small dish of moon water)
- Two green candles for growth and friendship
- A piece of rose quartz for love and harmony in friendships
- Basil and cinnamon, herbs associated with friendship and connection
- A piece of paper and a pen to write down qualities you value in a friendship
- A small pot with soil and seeds that symbolize the growth of new relationships (such as marigold for affection and joy)

Preparation:

1. Choose a time during the new moon when you can quietly reflect on your intentions.

2. Cleanse your space and the items you will use, perhaps with the smoke of sage or through visualization.

The Spell:

1. Light the two green candles, placing them on either side of your moon representation, to symbolize the potential of new or growing friendships.

2. Hold the rose quartz in your hand, infusing it with your desire for loving, harmonious friendships.

3. Write down the qualities you seek in a friend or wish to strengthen in your current friendships on the piece of paper.

4. Plant the seeds in the soil as you focus on planting the seeds of new friendships or the growth of current ones. As you cover them with soil, say, "Seeds of friendship, in this soil, grow strong and true, through joy and toil."

5. Sprinkle the basil and cinnamon over the pot, stating, "Basil for harmony, cinnamon for spice, may my friendships be nurturing and nice."

6. Place the rose quartz next to or in the pot, affirming, "Rose quartz, stone of heart, bless these friendships, never to part."

Sealing the Spell:

1. Spend a few moments meditating on the flame of the candles, imagining the warmth spreading to encompass all your current and future friendships.

2. Say, "By the new moon's light, so bright and thin, let new friendships come in, existing ones deepen, within."

3. Let the candles burn down safely or extinguish them, knowing that your intentions are set with the new moon.

After the Spell:

1. Water the seeds regularly, caring for them as you would nurture a friendship.

2. Carry the rose quartz with you or keep it in a place where you often socialize or meet new people.

3. Reflect on the qualities you wrote down, striving to embody them in your interactions.

4. As the seeds begin to sprout and grow, take it as a sign that your friendships are also growing and take time to reach out to friends old and new.

5. Keep a journal to note any new opportunities for friendship or deepening connections that arise following the spell.

This New Moon Friendship Spell harnesses the moon's phase of new beginnings to cultivate the fertile ground for blossoming friendships and enriched connections.

36. TOWER OF TRUST SPELL

Intent: To build a strong foundation of trust in a relationship, whether it's romantic, platonic, or professional, and to fortify the bonds of mutual respect and reliability.

You Will Need:
- A tower or stack of stones, which can be small pebbles or larger rocks, symbolizing the building of trust
- A blue candle for communication and trust
- Small slips of paper and a pen to write aspects of trust that are important to you
- A bowl of water with a pinch of salt, for purity and truth
- Lavender oil to promote calm and understanding
- A piece of lapis lazuli or blue lace agate, stones known for their properties of deepening trust and clarity in communication

Preparation:
1. Find a quiet space where you can focus on the intent of your spell without interruptions.
2. Cleanse your space, the stones, and other materials using sage smoke or visualization of a cleansing light.

The Spell:

1. Light the blue candle, and as you do, concentrate on the flame as a beacon for truth and clarity.

2. Write down different aspects of trust on the slips of paper—honesty, reliability, confidentiality, etc.

3. One by one, read each aspect aloud, and place a slip of paper under a stone as you begin to stack them, visualizing each stone representing the solidification of that aspect within the tower of trust you are building.

4. As you place each stone, chant, "Stone upon stone, trust is built, free from guilt, free from wilt."

5. Add a few drops of lavender oil to the bowl of saltwater, saying, "Lavender for peace, water for truth, clear the way for trust's smooth growth."

6. Gently anoint each stone with a touch of the lavender-infused water, reaffirming the purity and sincerity of your intentions.

7. Once your tower is built, place the lapis lazuli or blue lace agate at its base, and speak, "Stone of true blue, deepen trust, in all we say and all we do."

Sealing the Spell:

1. Take a moment to reflect on the tower you have built, each stone a commitment to maintain and honor trust.

2. Extinguish the candle, feeling the warm energy of trust enveloping your relationship, and say, "By this spell, may trust never rust, may it be strong as stone, and never alone."

After the Spell:

1. Leave the tower of stones in a place where you can see it daily as a reminder to uphold the trust you've cultivated.

2. Take the piece of lapis lazuli or blue lace agate with you when meeting with the person you wish to build trust with or keep it in a shared space between you.

3. Replace the saltwater back into the earth as a symbol of grounding your trust in reality.

4. Reflect on actions you can take to demonstrate trustworthiness, and journal any thoughts or experiences that relate to trust in your relationship following the spell.

With the Tower of Trust Spell, you set in motion the energies of steadfast trust and open communication, creating a durable and dependable foundation upon which your relationship can stand firm.

37. POPULARITY DRAWING OIL

Intent: To concoct an oil blend that, when worn, draws people towards you, enhancing your charisma, charm, and social appeal.

You Will Need:

- A base oil such as jojoba or sweet almond oil for your mixture
- Sunflower oil, for its associations with positivity and radiance
- Dried orange peel or a few drops of orange essential oil for its uplifting and attractive properties
- A small piece of high-quality vanilla bean or a few drops of vanilla essential oil for warmth and to attract good fortune
- Lavender buds or lavender essential oil for calm, approachability, and peace
- A small bottle or vial to hold your drawing oil
- A small funnel or pipette for transferring oils

Preparation:

1. Choose a space where you can work in peace and concentrate on your intentions.

2. Clean the area and your container thoroughly to ensure a pure blend.

The Spell:

1. Start by pouring the base oil into the bottle, filling it about halfway. This oil anchors your intentions and serves as the foundation for your blend.

2. Add the sunflower oil while visualizing yourself shining brightly, drawing people in with your positive energy.

3. Place the dried orange peel or add a few drops of orange essential oil into the mixture, focusing on the peel's ability to attract and the oil's quality to uplift and warm the spirits of those around you.

4. Introduce the vanilla bean or vanilla essential oil, and as you do, imagine the sweet aroma enhancing your social interactions, making you more desirable and well-liked.

5. Sprinkle in the lavender buds or add drops of lavender essential oil for peace and tranquility, ensuring that your popularity grows from genuine connections and positive experiences.

6. As you mix the oils, chant: "Oil blend, draw friends near and far, bring popularity, be it my shining star."

Sealing the Spell:

1. Cap the bottle and shake it gently, blending all the ingredients while focusing on your social goals.
2. Hold the bottle in your hands, warming it with your personal energy, and say, "With this oil, I draw others in, to bask in the light of charisma's win."
3. Store the bottle in a place where it can continue to absorb your intentions until you are ready to use it.

After the Spell:

1. Anoint yourself with the oil before social events, meetings, or whenever you wish to boost your social magnetism.
2. Keep the oil on hand for times when you need a quick confidence lift or when heading into social situations.
3. Record your observations and feelings about your social interactions and any increased popularity in your journal.
4. Recharge your intentions regularly by holding the bottle, visualizing your social desires, and affirming your intentions.

With this Popularity Drawing Oil, you have a magical aid to enhance your social presence, making you a beacon of charm and friendliness in your personal and professional circles.

38. SPELL TO FIND A LOST ITEM

Intent: To focus your energy and attention to locate a lost item, tapping into intuition and guidance to lead you to where the item has been misplaced.

You Will Need:

- A white candle for clarity and illumination
- A pendulum or a dowsing rod for divination purposes
- A picture or an object related to the lost item, if available
- A piece of paper and a pen to write down where you might find the item
- Sage or palo santo for smudging and to clear your mind
- A small charm or key to act as a symbolic 'finder'

Preparation:

1. Choose a quiet place where you can concentrate without distractions.
2. Cleanse the space, yourself, and the tools you will be using with the smoke of sage or palo santo.

The Spell:

1. Light the white candle, and as you do, set the intention to uncover the lost item with clarity and brightness.

2. If you have a picture or related object, place it in front of the candle as a visual aid for your search.

3. Write down the last places you remember having the item, or where it's often used or stored.

4. Hold the pendulum or dowsing rod, and ask it to guide you to the lost item. Visualize the item clearly in your mind.

5. Say aloud, "What is lost must now be found, take me there, safe and sound."

6. Allow the pendulum or rod to guide your movements, trusting in your intuition and the tools' ability to lead you.

Sealing the Spell:

1. Follow the pendulum or rod's guidance around your space, remaining open to intuition and any subtle signals.

2. When you feel drawn to a location, explore it thoroughly for the lost item.

3. Once you've found the item (or even if you need to take a break), snuff out the candle, thanking it for its

guiding light, and say, "The light has led me to what was lost, gratitude and relief, worth the cost."

After the Spell:

1. Keep the charm or key with you when you are looking for things in the future, as a reminder of your successful finding.
2. Reflect on the process in your journal, noting how the item was found and how the spell aided your search.
3. Consider performing a small ritual of thanks if the item is particularly important or cherished, acknowledging the role of the divine or your own intuition in its return.

This Spell to Find a Lost Item combines practical search techniques with magical guidance, helping to focus your mind and energy on recovering what has been misplaced.

39. CAR PROTECTION AND BLESSING

Intent: To safeguard your vehicle, ensuring it remains reliable, secure, and carries you to your destinations without harm.

You Will Need:

- A white candle for protection and purity
- A key charm or a small model car to represent your vehicle
- A piece of clear quartz for clear travels and safety
- A sprig of rosemary for mental clarity while driving and protection
- Sage to cleanse any negative energies from the vehicle
- A small bowl of water blessed with salt for purification
- An essential oil blend of frankincense for protection and peppermint for alertness

Preparation:

1. Find a quiet time to focus on your car and its well-being, free from distractions.
2. Cleanse your space and all the items you will use in the blessing.

The Spell:

1. Light the white candle, allowing its light to represent a protective shield around your car.

2. Hold the key charm or model car, and visualize your vehicle being enveloped in a protective light.

3. Pass the clear quartz over the flame gently, and then say, "Quartz crystal, guard my ride, ensure safety on every side."

4. Lay the sprig of rosemary next to the candle, and speak, "Rosemary for protection strong, keep my travels free from wrong."

5. Light the sage and waft its smoke over the key charm or model car, cleansing it of any negative energies.

6. Anoint the charm or model car with the saltwater, and say, "Water and salt, purify and protect, let my car no harm detect."

7. Dab a drop of the essential oil blend on the charm or model car for focus and protection while driving.

Sealing the Spell:

1. Hold the anointed charm or model car near the candle's flame (not too close) and declare, "By fire, water, earth, and air, let this spell fix my car in protective care."

2.   Allow the candle to burn down safely, or snuff it out, signifying the end of the ritual.

After the Spell:

1.   Attach the key charm to your car keys or place the model car in your vehicle as a talisman of protection.

2.   Every time you enter your car, take a moment to touch the charm or model and reaffirm your intent for safe and secure travels.

3.   Dispose of the rosemary and sage remains respectfully, returning them to the earth.

4.   Regularly renew the spell, especially if you feel the need for additional protection or after any long trips.

This Car Protection and Blessing spell is a spiritual maintenance routine that works in tandem with your physical upkeep to ensure your vehicle is always enveloped in protective energies.

40. PROTECTION SPELL BOTTLE

Intent: To create a protective amulet in the form of a spell bottle, which serves to guard the bearer from negative energies, psychic attacks, and malevolent intentions.

You Will Need:
- A small bottle or jar with a secure lid
- Salt, preferably black or Himalayan pink, for grounding and protection
- Iron filings or nails to ward off negativity and evil spirits
- Black tourmaline or obsidian, stones known for their protective properties
- White sage leaves, cedar, or bay leaves for cleansing and safeguarding
- Garlic skins or cloves for banishment of evil and shielding
- A white candle for sealing the bottle and purity of intent
- Red ribbon to tie around the bottle, symbolizing strength and power

Preparation:

1. Select a peaceful area to work where you won't be disturbed.

2. Cleanse the space, the bottle, and the ingredients with sage smoke or your chosen method to purify them before use.

The Spell:

1. Begin by placing a layer of salt at the bottom of the bottle, setting a pure and protective foundation.

2. Add the iron filings or nails, envisioning them as a barrier that repels negative influences.

3. Place the black tourmaline or obsidian into the bottle, affirming their power to shield and protect.

4. Put the sage leaves, cedar, or bay leaves in next, saying, "Herbs of protection, cleanse and guard, let no harm enter, let all ill be barred."

5. Add the garlic skins or cloves while chanting, "Garlic that wards, protect this place, and shield the bearer from ill with grace."

6. Seal the bottle with its lid and drip the white candle's wax over the seal to ensure it's closed tight.

7. Wrap the red ribbon around the bottle, tying it while declaring, "With this ribbon, I bind the power, in this bottle, safety towers."

Sealing the Spell:

1. Hold the sealed bottle close, and visualize it glowing with a bright, protective light.

2. Recite, "This spell is sealed, this charm is made, within this bottle, protection's laid."

3. Blow out the candle, signifying the end of the ritual and the setting of your intention.

After the Spell:

1. Keep the Protection Spell Bottle near your entrance to safeguard your home, or carry it with you for personal protection.

2. Whenever you feel the need for an extra layer of protection, hold the bottle, reaffirming your belief in its power.

3. Renew the spell annually, or whenever you feel necessary, by replacing the contents and resealing the bottle.

4. Reflect on the sense of security the bottle provides and note any shifts in the energy around you.

This Protection Spell Bottle serves as a potent safeguard, combining physical materials with your intent to create a powerful talisman against negativity.

41. WELL-BEING MIRROR SPELL

Intent: To use the reflective and revealing properties of a mirror to affirm personal well-being, self-acceptance, and to reflect negative energies away from you.

You Will Need:
- A small mirror, clean and unblemished
- Sea salt for purification
- A white candle for clarity and purification
- Lavender oil for tranquility and positive energy
- Rose petals to enhance self-love and confidence
- Clear quartz to amplify your intentions
- A piece of paper and a pen to write affirmations of well-being

Preparation:
1. Find a quiet space where you can be reflective and undisturbed.
2. Cleanse the area, the mirror, and your other materials with the smoke of sage or your preferred method.

The Spell:

1. Light the white candle, focusing on its flame as a beacon of purity and wellness.

2. Lay the mirror flat before you, and sprinkle a circle of sea salt around it, stating, "Circle of salt, protect and purify, let only love and good reflect here by."

3. Write your affirmations of well-being on the paper, focusing on positive attributes and your intent for health and happiness.

4. Anoint the corners of the mirror with lavender oil while chanting, "Oil of lavender, calm and serene, bring well-being, let it be seen."

5. Place the rose petals on the mirror's surface, and say, "Petals of rose, with beauty and grace, enhance my wellness, in this space."

6. Hold the clear quartz over the candle flame (carefully) and then the mirror, affirming, "Quartz so clear, amplify my intent, reflect well-being, and prevent dissent."

7. Set your written affirmations under the mirror, allowing them to be 'reflected' back to you.

Sealing the Spell:

1. Gaze into the mirror, seeing yourself surrounded by the light of the candle and the positive energy you've summoned.

2. Recite the affirmations aloud while looking into your own eyes, deeply accepting each word.

3. Blow out the candle, envisioning the extinguishing of any negative energy or self-doubt.

4. Say, "By this spell, I claim my power, wellness and peace bloom like a flower."

After the Spell:

1. Hang the mirror in a place where you'll see it daily, and pause to reaffirm your well-being each time you pass by.

2. Carry the rose petals and quartz with you, or place them where you'll see them often to remind you of your spell and intentions.

3. Keep the affirmations in a journal or a place where you can read them regularly.

4. Renew the spell periodically, especially during times of stress or ill health, to reinforce the positive energies around your well-being.

This Well-Being Mirror Spell serves as a daily reaffirmation of your personal strength and happiness, mirroring back to you the best of who you are and aspire to be.

42. POSITIVITY INCENSE

Intent: To create a blend of incense that when burned, purifies the atmosphere, dispelling negative energies and infusing your space with positivity and uplifting vibrations.

You Will Need:
- Dried lavender for peace and tranquility
- Dried rose petals for positive emotions and love
- Frankincense resin for purification and spiritual upliftment
- Citrus peel, dried or fresh, for brightness and joy
- A mortar and pestle to blend your herbs and resins
- A charcoal disc for burning your incense
- A fireproof dish or incense burner

Preparation:
1. Set the mood for your preparation by ensuring the space is clean, calm, and comfortable.
2. Ground yourself and focus on your intent to bring positivity into your life and surroundings.

The Spell:

1. In your mortar and pestle, start by grinding the lavender, releasing its calming scent and envisioning its soothing properties permeating your space.

2. Add the rose petals, gently crushing them, and as you do, imagine the air filling with the essence of love and happiness.

3. Sprinkle the frankincense resin into the mix, picturing it cleansing and sanctifying the air as it will burn.

4. Include the citrus peel, whether grated fresh or dried, to inject a burst of joyful energy into your blend.

5. Grind and mix all your ingredients while focusing on your intention, and chant, "Blend of joy, blend of light, cast away the shades of night."

6. Once your incense is blended, light the charcoal disc in your fireproof dish or burner until it's glowing red and sprinkle a pinch of your incense on top.

Sealing the Spell:

1. As the incense begins to smolder and the aromatic smoke rises, visualize it filling the room, dispersing negativity and brightening the energy.

2. Move around your space, if desired, spreading the smoke to all corners, while affirming, "Smoke rise and spread far and wide, bring positivity inside."

3. Allow the incense to burn out naturally, letting its aroma and energies set the tone for a positive and peaceful environment.

After the Spell:

1. Store any leftover incense in a jar or a pouch, keeping it in a place where it can maintain its vibrancy.

2. Use the incense regularly, especially when you feel the need to lift your spirits or during meditation and reflection.

3. Note the changes in your mood and the atmosphere in your journal, recognizing the beneficial effects of your positivity incense.

This Positivity Incense Spell calls upon the natural properties of herbs and resins to create a sanctuary of good vibes, allowing you to foster a consistently positive and serene environment.

43. MONEY KNOT SPELL

Intent: To attract financial prosperity and create a continuous flow of wealth through the symbolic act of tying knots.

You Will Need:
- Three green candles for growth and money
- A green ribbon or cord, which symbolizes money coming towards you
- Cinnamon oil for quick success and financial rewards
- Nine coins of any denomination to represent wealth
- A piece of paper and a pen to write down your financial goals

Preparation:
1. Find a space where you can focus on your financial intentions without distractions.
2. Cleanse the area, the candles, ribbon, and coins to ensure they are free of any previous energies.

The Spell:
1. Light the green candles in a triangle formation, setting the stage for wealth and prosperity.

2. Anoint the ribbon with cinnamon oil, focusing on your intention to attract financial success quickly.

3. Write your financial goals on the piece of paper. Place it in the center of the candle triangle.

4. Lay the coins in a row in front of you, and as you pick up each one, state an aspect of wealth you wish to attract (such as "abundance", "stability", "generosity").

5. Begin to tie knots in the green ribbon, evenly spacing them out. With each knot, chant, "Knot of one, the spell's begun. Knot of two, wealth comes true. Knot of three, money comes to me."

6. Continue with, "Knot of four, opportunity knocks at my door. Knot of five, my wealth thrives. Knot of six, this spell is fixed."

7. Finish with, "Knot of seven, success is given. Knot of eight, increase is great. Knot of nine, prosperity is mine."

8. Wrap the knotted ribbon around the coins and the written financial goals, binding them together.

Sealing the Spell:

1. Hold the bundled ribbon and coins between your palms, visualizing your financial aspirations manifesting into reality.

2. Say, "By knot and coin, by wax and flame, wealth and abundance come without blame."
3. Let the candles burn down safely, symbolizing the illumination of your path to financial success.

After the Spell:

1. Keep the knotted ribbon with coins in a safe place, preferably where you store your financial documents or near your workspace.
2. Whenever you see or touch the ribbon, reaffirm your intentions for financial prosperity.
3. Carry out practical financial actions that align with your goals, such as budgeting or investing, to ground the spell in reality.
4. Note any changes in your financial situation, unexpected gains, or new opportunities in your journal, recognizing the influence of your Money Knot Spell.

This Money Knot Spell combines the act of tying knots with the power of intention, creating a potent symbol for attracting and maintaining wealth.

44. PROSPERITY TALISMAN

Intent: To craft a talisman that draws abundance and financial success into your life, serving as a magnet for prosperity.

You Will Need:

- A small green pouch, symbolizing money and abundance
- Basil leaves, associated with wealth and success
- A piece of pyrite (also known as fool's gold) or a citrine crystal for their money-attracting properties
- A silver coin, to represent the flow of money
- Cinnamon, for quick financial benefits and luck
- Allspice berries, for added energy and determination in achieving prosperity
- A bay leaf to represent triumph and victory in financial endeavors
- A piece of paper and a pen to write down your financial intention or goal

Preparation:

1. Find a quiet space where you can concentrate on abundance without distractions.

2. Cleanse your space and materials, perhaps with the smoke of sage or through visualization, to prepare them for the ritual.

The Spell:

1. Write your financial goal or intention on the piece of paper, then fold it, focusing deeply on your wish for prosperity.

2. Place the folded paper in the bottom of the green pouch.

3. Add the basil leaves, while speaking aloud your desire for wealth and prosperity.

4. Take the pyrite or citrine and hold it in your hand, charging it with your intention. Place it in the pouch, affirming its role as a magnet for wealth.

5. Drop the silver coin into the pouch, symbolizing the attraction of money.

6. Sprinkle cinnamon over the contents of the pouch, for swift and positive financial success.

7. Add the allspice berries, to enhance your determination and to energize your intentions.

8. Lastly, place the bay leaf inside, as a symbol of victory and achievement.

Sealing the Spell:

1. Draw the strings of the pouch to close it, and as you do, visualize sealing your intention for prosperity within it.
2. Hold the closed pouch in both hands, and say, "Talisman of prosperity, bring wealth to me, as I will, so mote it be."
3. Keep the talisman in a safe place, such as your wallet, purse, or the wealth corner of your home (often the back left corner from the front door in Feng Shui).

After the Spell:

1. Regularly hold the talisman, reaffirming your intent for prosperity and visualizing your financial goals being met.
2. Carry out practical steps towards your financial goals, allowing the talisman to guide and enhance those efforts.
3. Reflect on the growth of your prosperity, noting any positive changes or manifestations of your intentions.

Your Prosperity Talisman is now charged with your intention, ready to assist you in attracting and maintaining abundance in your life.

45. MONEY GROW DRESSING OIL

Intent: To create an anointing oil that attracts financial growth and abundance, perfect for dressing candles in money spells or anointing objects like wallets and cash registers.

You Will Need:

- A base oil, such as olive oil or almond oil, known for its prosperity drawing properties
- Basil leaves or essential oil for attracting wealth
- Peppermint leaves or essential oil for financial success and purity of intention
- A pinch of ground cinnamon or a drop of cinnamon oil for quick and positive financial blessings
- A small piece of green aventurine or pyrite, stones known for attracting wealth
- A few chamomile flowers for relaxation and to attract money
- A glass bottle or vial to mix and store your oil
- A small funnel or pipette for transferring oils

Preparation:

1. Cleanse your space, all tools, and ingredients energetically to ensure they are ready to hold your intention for financial growth.
2. Ground yourself, focusing on the abundance you wish to attract into your life.

The Spell:

1. Begin by filling your glass bottle halfway with your base oil.
2. Add the basil, focusing on the wealth you wish to attract, and say, "Basil herb of wealth, infuse this oil with your prosperous health."
3. Introduce the peppermint, envisioning your financial pathways opening and clearing as you do, and affirm, "Peppermint crisp, bring financial gain, let my wealth grow without wane."
4. Sprinkle in the cinnamon, visualizing quick success in your financial endeavors, and chant, "Cinnamon spice, draw money fast, ensure my prosperity will last."
5. Place the green aventurine or pyrite in the bottle, allowing its energy to amplify your intentions.
6. Add the chamomile flowers, envisioning a calming energy that attracts wealth without stress, and say, "Chamomile bloom, draw money my way, let abundance come and stay."

7. Seal the bottle, and shake it gently, mixing the oil with the herbs, resins, and stones.

Sealing the Spell:

1. Hold the sealed bottle in your hands and visualize it glowing with a bright, golden light, symbolizing the growth of your finances.

2. Affirm, "With this oil, I dress and bless, may my money multiply and never be less."

3. Store the bottle in your wealth area or with your financial tools (like your wallet or chequebook).

After the Spell:

1. Anoint money-related objects like your wallet, purse, or piggy bank with the oil to draw in financial growth.

2. Dress candles used in money spells with the oil to enhance their effectiveness.

3. Regularly shake the bottle to reactivate the herbs and stones' energy.

4. Reflect on your financial progress, keeping an eye out for new opportunities and successes.

With your Money Grow Dressing Oil, you have a magical tool ready to enhance spells, anoint objects, and draw in the energies of wealth and abundance.

46. MILK AND HONEY MONEY BATH RITUAL

Intent: To immerse yourself in the energies of abundance and luxury, allowing the properties of milk and honey to attract wealth and prosperity into your life.

You Will Need:

- A bathtub filled with warm water
- A cup of milk (cow, goat, or a non-dairy alternative) symbolizing nourishment and abundance
- A quarter cup of local, raw honey for sweetness and wealth
- Gold or green candles to represent money and prosperity
- Basil leaves for attracting financial success
- A few drops of essential oils associated with wealth, such as bergamot, patchouli, or vetiver
- Rose petals to encourage love of self and of life's riches
- A small cloth bag or tea infuser with chamomile and mint, for relaxation and purification
- A coin or a small amount of currency to symbolize the wealth you're drawing towards yourself

Preparation:

1. Begin by cleaning the bathroom, creating a sacred space for your ritual.

2. Draw a bath with warm water, adjusting the temperature to your comfort.

The Ritual:

1. Light the gold or green candles around the tub, setting the intention for wealth and prosperity.

2. As you add the milk to the bathwater, visualize it filling the tub with the energy of abundance.

3. Pour the honey into the water, focusing on the sweetness and luxury it represents, and stir clockwise to distribute.

4. Sprinkle the basil leaves into the water, inviting the essence of success and financial growth.

5. Add the essential oils, drop by drop, visualizing each as a key unlocking the door to wealth.

6. Scatter the rose petals over the surface, acknowledging the love for the abundance you have and will receive.

7. Place the cloth bag or tea infuser containing chamomile and mint into the bath for a soothing and cleansing effect.

8. Hold the coin in your hand, then gently place it in the water, affirming your readiness to receive wealth.

Sealing the Ritual:

1. Step into the bath, immerse yourself, and relax as you soak, feeling the energies of prosperity enveloping you.
2. Visualize your financial goals being met, imagining your life filled with the wealth and abundance you desire.
3. When you're ready to emerge from the bath, blow out the candles, thanking them for their light and warmth.
4. Drain the water, envisioning any negativity or financial blockages being washed away.

After the Ritual:

1. Collect the coin, dry it off, and place it in your wallet or another space associated with your finances.
2. Dispose of the basil, chamomile, mint, and rose petals in a way that feels respectful and fitting.
3. Reflect on the feelings of abundance and prosperity, and carry that energy with you in the days ahead.

4. Consider writing a note of gratitude for what you have and what you will receive in your journal or a place you can revisit.

With the Milk and Honey Money Bath Ritual, you create a luxurious space to not only relax but to also align yourself with the frequencies of wealth and prosperity, fostering an environment where financial growth is welcomed and nurtured.

47. FORTUNE APPLE POMANDER SPELL

Intent: To craft a pomander that attracts fortune and positive energy into your home or personal space.

You Will Need:

- A fresh, firm apple as a symbol of abundance and the heart of your pomander
- Whole cloves to draw wealth and prosperity, and to preserve the apple
- A ribbon, preferably green for growth or gold for prosperity
- Cinnamon sticks or ground cinnamon for success and protection
- A small carving tool or toothpick to inscribe symbols into the apple
- A sprinkle of nutmeg to enhance the energy of fortune
- A circle of green fabric or a decorative plate to place your pomander on

Preparation:

1. Choose a quiet time where you can focus on crafting your pomander without interruptions.

2. Cleanse your workspace and all materials with your preferred method, such as sage smoke or visualization.

The Spell:

1. Begin by carving symbols of fortune, such as runes, sigils, or even dollar signs, into the apple with your tool or toothpick.
2. Push the whole cloves into the apple, covering it in a pattern or completely for a strong fragrance and preservation qualities.
3. Wrap the ribbon around the clove-studded apple, tying it with a bow to secure your intentions.
4. Place the cinnamon sticks or sprinkle ground cinnamon over the apple, saying, "Cinnamon for success, spice of fire, bring to me my heart's desire."
5. Dust the apple with nutmeg, invoking abundance and good luck, and chant, "Nutmeg's fortune, sweet and strong, to me, prosperity belongs."

Sealing the Spell:

1. Place the pomander on the circle of green fabric or the decorative plate, setting it in your chosen area to attract positive energy.

2. As you complete the arrangement, say, "Pomander of fortune, work your charm, bring to me wealth and cause no harm."

3. Visualize a golden light of abundance enveloping the pomander, radiating out to fill your space.

After the Spell:

1. Leave the pomander in a prominent place where you will see it daily, such as the living room, to remind you of your intention.

2. Refresh the pomander as needed, and when it begins to wither, replace it with a new one, repeating the spell to maintain the flow of fortune.

3. Reflect on the prosperity that comes into your life, noting new opportunities or financial gains that may arise after setting the pomander.

This Fortune Apple Pomander Spell serves as a fragrant and visual beacon of prosperity, combining the natural magic of herbs and symbols to create a potent charm for attracting good fortune.

48. CLEANSING DEBT WATER

Intent: To craft a ritual water for washing away financial debts and to cleanse oneself from the burdens of financial obligations.

You Will Need:
- A bowl of spring water as a base for your cleansing water
- A small handful of basil leaves for attracting financial prosperity and for its cleansing properties
- Fresh mint leaves for financial wisdom and abundance
- A sliver of lemon peel for purification and to clear away debt
- A piece of clear quartz to amplify your intentions
- A green candle to symbolize money and prosperity
- A piece of paper and a pen to write down your debts or financial worries

Preparation:
1. Find a quiet place where you can concentrate on the ritual without interruption.
2. Cleanse your space, the bowl, and your ingredients, using sage smoke or by placing them in sunlight or moonlight for a few hours.

The Ritual:

1. Light the green candle, setting the intention for wealth and financial balance.

2. Write down your debts or financial concerns on the piece of paper. Fold it and place it underneath the bowl.

3. Add the basil leaves to the spring water, stating, "Basil, herb of wealth, cleanse my debts and restore financial health."

4. Place the mint leaves into the water, affirming, "Mint, bring abundance my way, provide the means for debts to pay."

5. Squeeze the lemon peel over the bowl, releasing its oils, and declare, "Lemon peel, cleanse my woes, clear my debts as this water flows."

6. Drop the clear quartz into the bowl, envisioning it energizing the water with your intentions.

Sealing the Ritual:

1. Stir the water clockwise with your fingers, visualizing your debts dissolving and your financial slate being wiped clean.

2. Say, "With this water, debts be gone, financial freedom, I draw upon."

3. Allow the green candle to burn down safely while you meditate on your intention.

After the Ritual:

1. Use the Cleansing Debt Water to lightly sprinkle on your wallet, credit cards, or financial statements, visualizing each as being cleared of debt.
2. Keep the clear quartz near your financial documents or carry it with you when discussing financial matters.
3. Dispose of the lemon peel, basil, and mint by returning them to nature, burying them, or placing them in a compost.
4. Burn the piece of paper with your debts written on it (safely), symbolizing the release of these financial burdens from your life.
5. Regularly remind yourself of the ritual by touching the water or the clear quartz, reinforcing your commitment to financial clarity.

This Cleansing Debt Water ritual is a symbolic act, helping to shift your mindset towards abundance and financial freedom, and away from the stress of debts and financial obligations.

49. PROSPERITY WALL HANGING

Intent: To create a decorative piece that serves as a daily visual affirmation of wealth, success, and continuous prosperity.

You Will Need:

- A wooden stick or dowel to serve as the foundation of the hanging
- Green and gold ribbons to symbolize money and success
- Cinnamon sticks for attracting swift financial blessings
- Small coins to represent the flow of wealth
- Jade or aventurine beads for their prosperity-attracting properties
- A golden thread or yarn for assembly
- Feathers to represent freedom and the idea that wealth will provide more opportunities
- A glue gun or another strong adhesive to secure items
- Scissors for cutting ribbons and thread

Preparation:

1. Choose a space where you can craft your wall hanging peacefully.

2. Clear your materials and workspace energetically, perhaps with a prayer or a moment of silence, focusing on your intent.

The Spell:

1. Begin by cutting lengths of green and gold ribbons, considering each cut as a financial goal or milestone you wish to achieve.

2. Tie the ribbons along the wooden stick or dowel, alternating colors, and as you do, say, "Green for growth, gold for gain, let prosperity flow like rain."

3. Glue cinnamon sticks to some of the ribbons, and as you attach each one, chant, "Cinnamon stick, spice of luck, make my wealth quick to unstuck."

4. String coins and jade or aventurine beads onto the golden thread, then attach these to the dowel, envisioning financial opportunities coming your way.

5. Affix feathers to the hanging, symbolizing the lightness and freedom that prosperity can bring.

6. As you work, visualize the completed wall hanging as a magnet, drawing wealth and success into your home and life.

Sealing the Spell:

1. Once your wall hanging is assembled, hold it up in front of you and say, "Prosperity hangs before me, as I will, so shall it be."

2. Hang your new prosperity talisman in a prominent place in your home, such as your living room, office, or even near the front door.

After the Spell:

1. Look at and touch the wall hanging daily, reinforcing the intent and belief in your financial goals and the prosperity you deserve.

2. Whenever you achieve a financial milestone, consider adding another ribbon, bead, or coin to the hanging, acknowledging your success and keeping the energy flowing.

3. Keep the space around the hanging clear and vibrant, allowing the energy of abundance to circulate freely.

4. Reflect on the changes in your financial situation since hanging the talisman, recording any shifts or successes in your journal.

This Prosperity Wall Hanging not only beautifies your space but also acts as a powerful visual and energetic tool to attract and maintain a state of wealth and financial success.

50. MONEY ENVELOPE TIME SPELL

Intent: To create a time-bound spell that gradually increases the flow of money into your life, symbolically sealed and set to manifest by a certain date.

You Will Need:

- A green envelope to represent money and financial growth
- Basil leaves for attracting financial success
- Three coins of increasing denominations to symbolize growing wealth
- A piece of paper and a pen to write your financial intention or the amount you wish to attract
- A cinnamon stick for quick and positive financial blessings
- A calendar or planner to choose a specific date for your intention to manifest
- A green candle to seal the envelope and represent the growth of wealth

Preparation:

1. Choose a quiet place where you can concentrate on the spell without interruptions.

2. Cleanse your materials with sage smoke or your preferred method, focusing on the energy of abundance.

The Spell:

1. Write your financial goal or the specific amount of money you wish to attract on the piece of paper.
2. Place the basil leaves, coins, and cinnamon stick inside the green envelope, laying them on top of your written financial goal.
3. Visualize each item radiating energy and power towards your financial intention.
4. Light the green candle, and let a few drops of wax fall onto the flap of the envelope, sealing your intentions within.
5. While the wax is still warm, press the envelope closed, and say, "With this seal, I mark the growth of wealth, to manifest by (state your chosen date)."
6. Blow out the candle, affirming the process in your mind.

Sealing the Spell:

1. Place the sealed envelope in a safe and undisturbed space where you will remember to retrieve it, such as

in your desk, a special box, or taped behind a framed picture related to wealth or success.

2. Mark the calendar or planner with the date you've chosen for the spell to come to fruition.

After the Spell:

1. Work towards your financial goal with real-world actions, knowing that the spell is supporting your efforts from the background.

2. On the chosen date, retrieve the envelope. Open it to release the energy, and give thanks for the abundance that has come into your life.

3. Count any money you have received since the spell was cast, recognizing it as a manifestation of your intention.

4. If you feel the need, you can repeat the spell for a new goal or to reinforce the current one, reflecting on the successes and learning from the experiences of the previous spell.

The Money Envelope Time Spell serves as a magical savings bond, maturing to bring you prosperity and financial gains by the time and date of your choosing.

51. MONEY MANIFESTATION CRYSTAL GRID

Intent: To harness the natural energies of crystals in a geometric pattern to create a powerful vortex for attracting and manifesting wealth.

You Will Need:

- A piece of cloth or paper with a grid pattern drawn on it, or you can use a wooden board specifically designed for crystal grids
- A central crystal, often a larger point or cluster, such as clear quartz or citrine, to amplify energy and intention
- Surrounding stones such as pyrite for wealth, green aventurine for prosperity, and tiger's eye for money-drawing power
- Smaller quartz points to direct energy inward or outward, depending on your intention
- Optional: gold flakes, coins, or symbols of wealth to place on or around the grid
- A piece of paper and a pen to write down your financial goal

Preparation:

1. Find a quiet space where you can lay out your grid and work without disturbances.

2. Cleanse your chosen area, the grid base, and all of your crystals with sage, palo santo, or moonlight.

The Spell:

1. Write your financial goal on the piece of paper and place it in the center of your grid base.

2. Set your central crystal on top of the written goal, envisioning it as a beacon, radiating your intention into the universe.

3. Begin placing your surrounding stones in a circular pattern or in the specific geometry of your grid. As you place each stone, focus on its financial attraction properties and your desire for wealth.

4. Point your smaller quartz points towards the central stone to direct energy inward, concentrating on manifesting, or outward to spread your intention far and wide.

5. If you're using additional symbols of wealth like gold flakes or coins, arrange them in a way that feels intuitive and powerful to you.

6. As you complete the setup, visualize the entire grid glowing with a golden light, pulsating with the potential to manifest wealth.

Sealing the Spell:

1. With your grid assembled, place your hands over it, not touching but hovering, and say, "Crystals of wealth, stones of power, bring to me financial strength this hour."

2. Visualize a golden light emerging from the grid, intertwining with the energy of your written intention, creating a dynamic field of attraction.

3. Leave the grid undisturbed, allowing it to work continuously on manifesting your financial goals.

After the Spell:

1. Regularly cleanse and re-energize your grid, especially during full moons or when you feel its energy needs refreshing.

2. Meditate with your grid, reinforcing your visualization of financial success and the flow of abundance into your life.

3. Take practical steps towards your financial goals to aid the manifestation process.

4. Document any financial successes or opportunities that arise, acknowledging the power and influence of your Money Manifestation Crystal Grid.

This Money Manifestation Crystal Grid acts as a powerful anchor for your intentions, drawing upon the synergistic energies of crystals to invite prosperity and financial abundance into your life.

52. NINE-DAY MONEY CANDLE SPELL

Intent: To perform a sustained candle ritual over nine days to gradually build energy and intention, drawing wealth and abundance into your life.

You Will Need:

- Nine green candles, symbolizing money and growth
- A plate or tray to hold the candles safely
- A coin to represent the wealth you want to attract
- Cinnamon oil or powder for swift financial blessings
- A small bowl of soil to represent growth and grounding of your financial intentions
- Basil leaves for prosperity
- A pen and paper to write down your financial goals or the amount you wish to manifest

Preparation:

1. Find a safe and quiet space where you can leave the candles burning undisturbed, such as on an altar or a dedicated table.
2. Cleanse the area and your materials with your preferred method, setting a pure space for the spell.

The Spell:

1. Write your financial goal or the amount of money you wish to attract on the piece of paper.

2. Anoint each candle with cinnamon oil or sprinkle them with cinnamon powder, focusing on your intention for quick and abundant financial rewards.

3. Place the paper with your financial goal underneath the plate or tray where you will arrange your candles.

4. Lay the coin on top of the paper as a symbol of the wealth you are drawing in.

5. Arrange the candles in a circle on the plate or tray, embedding them slightly in the bowl of soil to secure them and to symbolize the growth of your finances.

6. Sprinkle basil leaves around the candles for additional attraction of wealth.

The Ritual:

1. Each day for nine days, light one candle while focusing on your intention of wealth and abundance.

2. As the candle burns, meditate on your financial goals, visualizing them as already achieved.

3. After the meditation, let the candle burn down completely (if it's a small candle) or extinguish it after an hour or so (if it's a larger candle), always ensuring safety.

Sealing the Spell:

1. On the ninth day, after lighting the last candle, say, "Nine candles burn, so let it be, wealth come forth, as I decree."

2. Allow the final candle to burn down completely, symbolizing the full manifestation of your wealth intention.

After the Spell:

1. Collect the remains of the candles and the coin, and store them in a green pouch or a box as a keepsake of your ritual.

2. Keep the pouch or box in a place where you handle your financial matters, such as near your desk or where you keep your wallet.

3. Take action towards your financial goals to assist the spell's energy, such as budgeting, investing, or saving.

4. Reflect on any increases in your wealth or new financial opportunities that arise, recognizing them as the fruits of your magical work.

The Nine-Day Money Candle Spell is a process of building energy and focus, culminating in a strong intention set into the universe for your financial prosperity.

53. CONFIDENCE CHARM SACHET

Intent: To create a personal talisman in the form of a sachet, carrying herbs and symbols to bolster self-confidence and personal power.

You Will Need:

- A small yellow or gold cloth or bag, representing confidence, joy, and personal power
- A ribbon or string to tie the sachet, in a color that speaks to you of confidence and strength
- Sunflower seeds or petals for positivity and strength
- A small piece of carnelian or tiger's eye, crystals known for enhancing confidence
- Rosemary for mental clarity and remembrance of one's worth
- Lavender for calmness and assurance in one's own abilities
- A bay leaf upon which you have written your name or personal symbol of power
- A few drops of essential oil of orange or lemon for uplifting energy and courage

Preparation:

1. Find a quiet space where you can concentrate on the sachet without interruptions.

2. Cleanse your space and all materials, using smoke, sound, or another cleansing method to purify the energies.

The Spell:

1. Lay out your cloth or open your bag, and place it in front of you.

2. On the bay leaf, write your name or a personal symbol that represents strength and confidence for you. Place it in the center of the cloth or inside the bag.

3. Add the sunflower seeds or petals, envisioning yourself standing tall and confident in any situation.

4. Hold the carnelian or tiger's eye stone, warming it in your hands, and visualize it glowing with a bright light. As you place it in the sachet, affirm that it will enhance your personal power.

5. Sprinkle rosemary for mental clarity and an assured spirit, and lavender for a calm demeanor and inner peace.

6. Add a few drops of orange or lemon essential oil, imagining their scent invigorating your spirit and bolstering your confidence.

7. Gather the edges of the cloth or close the bag, and tie it shut with the ribbon or string while saying, "With this charm, I tie in strength, confidence within me grows at length."

Sealing the Spell:

1. Hold the completed sachet between your hands, focusing on your intention to be confident and powerful.

2. Say, "Sachet of power, sachet of might, bolster my spirit, enhance my light."

3. Carry the sachet with you, especially in situations where you need a boost of confidence or when engaging in personal development activities.

After the Spell:

1. Whenever you feel in need of an extra boost of confidence, hold the sachet, take deep breaths, and remember your own worth and strength.

2. Keep the sachet in a pocket, bag, or under your pillow, or hang it somewhere you will see it daily as a reminder of your capabilities.

3. Periodically refresh the sachet with new herbs, stones, or a few more drops of essential oil to maintain its potency.

4. Note any changes in your confidence levels or situations where you felt the sachet helped in your journal.

The Confidence Charm Sachet serves as a portable source of empowerment, infusing your aura with herbs and crystals that foster strength, courage, and self-assurance.

54. PROMOTION DREAM SPELL

Intent: To focus your subconscious mind on achieving a promotion or advancement in your career through the power of dreams.

You Will Need:
- A purple candle for ambition and power
- A small sachet or a piece of cloth to make a dream pillow
- Lavender for relaxation and ensuring a restful sleep
- Dried mugwort to enhance prophetic dreams and clarity
- Bay leaves to symbolize victory and success
- A small piece of paper and a pen to write down your career goals
- A few drops of essential oil of peppermint or rosemary for mental sharpness and memory

Preparation:
1. Select a quiet evening where you can perform the spell undisturbed and have a restful night's sleep afterward.

2. Cleanse your bedroom and the materials you will use in the spell to create a sacred space for your intentions.

The Spell:

1. Light the purple candle, and as it burns, focus on visualizing the promotion or career advancement you desire.

2. Write down your career goal on the piece of paper, fold it, and place it inside the sachet or in the center of the cloth.

3. Add the lavender to the sachet, intending for deep and restorative sleep.

4. Sprinkle in the dried mugwort, with the goal of enhancing your dreams and bringing clarity to the path ahead.

5. Place the bay leaves into the sachet, as a symbol of triumph and the success you will achieve.

6. Anoint the sachet with a few drops of peppermint or rosemary oil, invoking mental strength and the power to remember your dreams.

7. Close the sachet or tie the cloth with a string, keeping your written goals and herbs inside.

Sealing the Spell:

1. Hold the completed sachet between your hands and whisper, "Dreams of night, bring insight, let my aspirations come to light."
2. Place the sachet under your pillow or nearby where its scent and energy can influence your dreams.
3. Blow out the candle, releasing your intention into the universe, trusting that your dreams will guide the way.

After the Spell:

1. Keep a dream journal close to your bed to record any significant dreams, especially those that pertain to your career or personal growth.
2. Each night before you go to sleep, hold the sachet, reaffirming your intention to move forward in your career.
3. Reflect on any insights or symbols from your dreams that could guide your actions towards achieving your promotion.
4. Regularly update or refresh the sachet with new herbs or oils to keep it potent, and repeat the spell as needed.

This Promotion Dream Spell taps into the power of your dreams to align your subconscious mind with your career aspirations, helping pave the way for professional success and recognition.

55. WORKPLACE PEACE SPELL

Intent: To foster a harmonious environment at work, easing tensions and encouraging cooperative and positive interactions among colleagues.

You Will Need:

- A blue candle for tranquility and peace
- Amethyst crystals for their calming energy and ability to promote harmony
- A small bowl of water to symbolize emotional clarity and peace
- Essential oil of lavender or chamomile for relaxation and stress relief
- Rose quartz to encourage understanding and empathy among coworkers
- A sprig of mint to promote clear communication and positive dialogue
- A piece of paper and a pen to write down your intention for peace in the workplace

Preparation:

1. Find a quiet time, ideally before you go to work, to perform this spell.

2. Cleanse your workspace, the materials, and yourself to ensure a pure setting for the spell.

The Spell:

1. Light the blue candle, focusing on its flame as a source of calm and peace for your workplace.

2. Write your intention for a peaceful work environment on the piece of paper, then fold it and place it underneath the bowl of water.

3. Add a few drops of lavender or chamomile essential oil to the bowl of water, and say, "Waters of peace, flow through my day, ease the tension, wash stress away."

4. Place the amethyst crystals around the candle, envisioning their soothing energy spreading to every corner of your workplace.

5. Submerge the rose quartz in the bowl of water, affirming its ability to foster understanding and empathy among all who work with you.

6. Lay the sprig of mint next to the bowl or float it on the water, chanting, "Mint for clear thoughts, mint for kind words, let peace fly in like the song of birds."

Sealing the Spell:

1. Visualize the atmosphere of your workplace infused with the calm, peaceful energy emanating from your spell components.

2. Say, "By candle, crystal, water, and herb, let peace in the workplace be undisturbed."

3. Let the candle burn safely for a while, reinforcing the peaceful energy you've conjured.

After the Spell:

1. Carry the rose quartz and a piece of the amethyst with you to work as a personal talisman of peace.

2. Dispose of the mint leaves respectfully after your workday, symbolizing the release of any negative energy.

3. Keep the bowl of scented water in your home as a reminder of your intention, and refresh it daily until you feel a change in your work environment.

4. Record any changes in the workplace atmosphere or in the interactions with your colleagues in your journal.

The Workplace Peace Spell aims to create a serene and cooperative atmosphere at work, making the environment more enjoyable and productive for everyone involved.

56. COWORKER COMMUNICATION SPELL

Intent: To enhance open and effective communication with a coworker, easing misunderstandings and promoting a clear exchange of ideas.

You Will Need:

- A blue candle for clear communication and understanding
- A small piece of paper to write down the name of the coworker or the communication goals
- A clear quartz crystal to amplify communication energies
- A sprig of rosemary for mental clarity and remembrance
- Honey, to sweeten interactions and speech
- Lavender for calm discussions and stress relief
- A feather to symbolize the lightness and ease of good communication
- A small cloth pouch or envelope to hold the items

Preparation:

1. Find a quiet space where you can focus on your intent without interruptions.

2. Cleanse your space and materials, readying them for the spell.

The Spell:

1. Light the blue candle, visualizing its light breaking through any communication barriers.

2. Write the name of your coworker or your communication goals on the piece of paper. Fold it and place it in front of the candle.

3. Place the clear quartz crystal on the paper, focusing on its energy to enhance and magnify your communication intentions.

4. Lay the sprig of rosemary next to or on top of the paper, invoking clarity of mind and memory for effective communication.

5. Drizzle a small amount of honey over the rosemary, intending to sweeten your words and interactions.

6. Place lavender around the base of the candle to create a peaceful environment for conversation.

7. Hold the feather, and let it lightly touch the candle flame (without catching fire) and then the items, symbolizing the ease with which your communications will flow.

Sealing the Spell:
1. Gather the items and place them inside the cloth pouch or envelope, saying, "With these tokens, I weave the spell, for open talks and clarity to dwell."
2. Snuff out the candle, affirming the sealing of your communication spell.

After the Spell:
1. Keep the pouch or envelope with you during interactions with the coworker or in a place where communication occurs, such as near your phone or computer.
2. Before engaging in discussions, hold the pouch and take deep breaths, visualizing positive and clear exchanges.
3. Reflect on the interactions with your coworker, noting improvements and areas for growth.
4. Renew the spell components periodically, especially before important meetings or discussions.

This Coworker Communication Spell focuses on fostering healthy dialogue, ensuring that both parties are heard and understood, thus improving professional relationships and teamwork.

57. ENERGIZING SPELL

Intent: To create an energetic boost that revitalizes your body and mind, providing you with the vigor and zest needed for your daily activities.

You Will Need:

- A red candle for vitality and energy
- A small piece of ginger root for its energizing properties
- A carnelian stone for stimulation and motivation
- Peppermint leaves or oil for mental clarity and alertness
- A citrus fruit, such as an orange or lemon, for invigoration and freshness
- A bowl of water to symbolize the flow of energy
- A sprig of rosemary for mental focus and memory enhancement

Preparation:

1. Find a time and place where you won't be disturbed, preferably in the morning to start your day with energy.

2. Clear your space of any negative energy and clutter to make room for the vibrant new energy you will be inviting.

The Spell:

1. Light the red candle, envisioning its flame igniting the fire of vitality within you.

2. Hold the ginger root in your hands, feeling its spicy energy, and say, "Ginger root, warm and bright, fill me with your dynamic light."

3. Place the carnelian stone near the candle, and imagine it pulsing with a motivating force.

4. Add the peppermint leaves to the bowl of water or dab a few drops of peppermint oil in it, focusing on the crisp, clean energy it represents.

5. Squeeze the citrus fruit gently, allowing a few drops of juice to fall into the water, and inhale its refreshing scent. Declare, "Citrus bright, with sunny zest, invigorate me to do my best."

6. Dip the rosemary sprig into the water, and then pass it through the candle's flame (carefully, to avoid burning it), speaking, "Rosemary for remembrance, let my mind be sharp and my body resilient."

Sealing the Spell:

1. Sprinkle a few droplets of the energized water onto
    your wrists or the back of your neck, feeling the
    refreshing and invigorating sensation.
2. Say, "With this spell, I summon energy, for all-day
    vitality, so mote it be!"
3. Extinguish the candle safely, locking in the vibrant
    energies you've raised.

After the Spell:

1. Carry the carnelian stone with you throughout the
    day to maintain the energetic boost.
2. Keep the ginger root on your desk, in your pocket, or in
    your workspace as a constant source of natural energy.
3. Dispose of the rosemary and citrus peels in a way that
    feels respectful, such as returning them to the earth.
4. Drink a glass of water with a slice of the remaining
    citrus to hydrate and continue the theme of
    invigoration from within.
5. Note how you feel energetically throughout the day,
    acknowledging the spell's impact on your vigor and
    alertness.

This Energizing Spell aims to fill you with a natural, sustained
energy, using the synergistic power of herbs, stones, and
intention to awaken your senses and revitalize your spirit.

58. SMOOTHING-OVER POWDER

Intent: To create a magical powder to help ease tensions, resolve conflicts, and encourage peaceful interactions, especially useful in smoothing over past disagreements or misunderstandings.

You Will Need:
- A mortar and pestle for grinding your ingredients
- Cornstarch or rice flour as a base for your powder
- Dried lavender for calm and peaceful energy
- Chamomile flowers to soothe anger and stress
- Rose petals to encourage harmony and understanding
- A pinch of sugar to sweeten thoughts and communication
- A small jar or container to store your powder

Preparation:
1. Find a quiet space where you can focus on your intentions without being disturbed.
2. Cleanse your space and materials, readying them to absorb your positive intent.

The Spell:

1. Begin by grounding the cornstarch or rice flour into your mortar and pestle, setting your intention for peace and tranquility.

2. Gradually add the dried lavender, crushing it into the base while visualizing its calming energy permeating the mixture.

3. Incorporate the chamomile flowers, focusing on their ability to diffuse anger and bring about relaxation.

4. Crush the rose petals into the blend, inviting feelings of harmony and mutual understanding.

5. Sprinkle in a pinch of sugar, with the intention of sweetening the attitudes and words of those who come into contact with the powder.

6. Mix all the ingredients thoroughly, while chanting softly, "Herbs of peace, mix and blend, bring conflicts to a gentle end."

Sealing the Spell:

1. Transfer the completed powder into your jar, and seal it with the lid.

2. Hold the jar in your hands, and say, "With this powder, I set the scene for peaceful talks, where strife has been."

3. Store the powder in a place where it can continue to charge with your intent, such as a windowsill bathed in sunlight or moonlight.

After the Spell:

1. Lightly dust areas where communication occurs, such as over a desk, a phone, or a doorway. If using in a shared space, ensure it is done respectfully and without causing disturbance.

2. Carry a bit of the powder with you, and when needed, discreetly sprinkle a small amount where you'll be interacting with others.

3. Before engaging in conversations you wish to go smoothly, pinch a bit of the powder and release it to the winds, visualizing your words and interactions flowing effortlessly and harmoniously.

4. Reflect on any positive changes in your interactions or the resolution of past conflicts, and note these in your journal.

The Smoothing-Over Powder spell is designed to subtly shift the energies around communication, making it a valuable tool for creating a more harmonious environment and mending relationships.

59. FULFILLMENT SCRYING

Intent: To use the ancient practice of scrying to gain insight into how you can achieve personal fulfillment and understand the steps needed to reach your goals.

You Will Need:

- A scrying mirror, a bowl of water, or a crystal ball, depending on your preference for scrying
- A quiet room where you will not be disturbed
- A journal or notepad for recording insights and revelations
- Incense or essential oil diffuser with a scent that promotes relaxation and openness, such as sandalwood or frankincense
- A comfortable seat or cushion to sit on while scrying
- Indirect lighting to avoid reflections and distractions on the scrying surface

Preparation:

1. Set up your scrying tool in the quiet room, placing it on a stable surface before your seat.
2. Dim the lights or arrange the lighting to minimize glare on the scrying surface.

3. Light the incense or start the diffuser to fill the room with a scent that aids in relaxation and psychic openness.

4. Sit comfortably before your scrying tool, and take several deep breaths to center yourself.

The Spell:

1. Gaze into your scrying surface, allowing your eyes to relax and lose focus slightly.

2. Set the intention silently or aloud: "Reveal to me the path to fulfillment, show me the steps I must take."

3. Remain open to whatever images, symbols, or feelings come to you. Don't force it; let the impressions flow naturally.

4. If your mind wanders, gently bring your focus back to the scrying surface and your intention.

Sealing the Spell:

1. Once you feel the session is complete or if you've received a significant insight, take a moment to ground yourself. You can do this by focusing on your breath, feeling the weight of your body in your seat, or visualizing roots growing from your feet into the ground.

2. Thank your scrying tool and any higher powers you believe in for the guidance provided.

3. Blow out the incense or turn off the diffuser, and turn the lights back on if you had them dimmed.

After the Spell:

1. Immediately write down any insights, symbols, or feelings that came to you during your scrying session. The act of writing can often bring additional clarity.

2. Reflect on what you've written and how it might apply to your current life situation and the pursuit of your goals.

3. Pay attention to your dreams in the nights following your scrying, as the insights may continue to unfold.

4. Repeat the scrying session as needed, but give yourself time to process and act on the information received before doing so again.

Fulfillment Scrying can be a powerful way to tap into your subconscious and the universal consciousness, revealing the path to personal success and satisfaction.

60. QUITTING SPELL OIL

Intent: To create an anointing oil that supports the process of quitting a bad habit or addiction, providing strength and determination.

You Will Need:

- A base oil, such as olive or coconut oil, for its health-affirming properties
- Black pepper essential oil for courage and overcoming negative habits
- Lavender for calmness and stress relief during the process
- Rosemary for mental clarity and remembrance of your reasons for quitting
- Amethyst crystals for their ability to promote sobriety and clarity
- A small bottle or vial to hold your oil
- A small funnel or pipette for transferring oils
- A label and pen to mark your Quitting Spell Oil

Preparation:

1. Find a quiet space where you can prepare your oil without interruptions.

2. Cleanse your workspace and materials with your preferred method to ensure they're free of residual energies.

The Spell:

1. Pour the base oil into your bottle, filling it about three-quarters of the way.

2. Add a few drops of black pepper essential oil, focusing on the strength and endurance it represents.

3. Introduce lavender oil to the blend, envisioning a soothing and calming effect enveloping you.

4. Sprinkle in a few drops of rosemary oil, affirming mental clarity and the power to make positive decisions.

5. Place the amethyst crystals near the bottle or, if small enough, inside it, to aid in warding off addictive behaviors and enhancing willpower.

6. Cap the bottle and shake it gently to mix the oils while focusing on your intention to quit your negative habit.

7. Label the bottle with its purpose and the date of creation.

Sealing the Spell:

1. Hold the bottle between your hands, close your eyes, and say, "With this oil, I anoint my skin, and with each touch, new strength begins."

2. Store the oil in a place where it will be easily accessible throughout your journey to quit your habit.

After the Spell:

1. Whenever you feel the urge related to your habit, apply a small amount of the oil to your wrists or temples, repeating your intention to quit and drawing on the oil's energy for support.

2. Reapply the oil as part of your morning routine to start each day with a reinforced commitment to your goal.

3. Keep a journal to track your progress, noting moments when the oil helped you resist temptation.

4. Refresh the oil as needed, especially if you feel its energy waning or after significant milestones in your journey to quit your habit.

The Quitting Spell Oil acts as both a physical and spiritual aid in your endeavor to overcome challenging habits and embrace a healthier lifestyle.

61. RESTORE LOVE KNOT SPELL

Intent: To reignite passion and affection in a relationship that has cooled or to mend the bonds of love that have been strained.

You Will Need:

- A pink candle for romance and affection
- A red candle for passion and deep love
- Two lengths of ribbon, one pink and one red, to represent different aspects of love
- Rose oil for love and healing heartaches
- Rose quartz to symbolize unconditional love and emotional healing
- A photograph or personal item from each person in the relationship
- A small cloth bag or a piece of soft fabric to store the knotted ribbons
- Lavender for harmony and tranquility in the relationship

Preparation:

1. Find a quiet and private space where you can focus on the spell without interruptions.

2. Cleanse your space, the candles, ribbons, and any other items you will use in the spell, setting a pure and loving intention.

The Spell:

1. Anoint both candles with rose oil, and as you do so, focus on your desire for restored love and connection.

2. Light the pink candle and the red candle, placing them side by side to symbolize the partnership you wish to bless.

3. Hold the two lengths of ribbon together, and as you tie the first knot, visualize the first time you felt love for your partner.

4. As you tie seven knots along the ribbons, think about different happy moments in the relationship, and with each knot say, "With this knot, I rebind our love, restore the connection, as below so above."

5. Lay the rose quartz between the two candles and place the photograph or personal items next to it, infusing the objects with loving energy.

6. Sprinkle the lavender around the candles, inviting a return to harmony and understanding.

7.   Once the knots are tied, pass the ribbons through the candle flames quickly without burning them, sealing the intent with fire's transformative energy.

Sealing the Spell:

1.   Place the knotted ribbons and rose quartz inside the cloth bag, along with the lavender.

2.   Close the bag and hold it to your heart, saying, "Love's warmth rekindled, love's bond healed, let this love be fully revealed."

3.   Let the candles burn down safely, symbolizing the rekindling of love and affection.

After the Spell:

1.   Keep the cloth bag in a place where you and your partner spend happy times together, or under the mattress to symbolize closeness.

2.   Whenever a challenge arises, hold the bag, remember the knots and their associated happy memories, and focus on the feelings of love and warmth.

3.   Work on practical ways to improve your relationship, knowing the spell has set positive intentions.

4. Renew the spell on an anniversary or special occasion, or during a new or full moon, to reinforce the bonds of love.

The Restore Love Knot Spell uses the power of intention, memory, and symbolic action to weave together the strands of affection and passion that may have loosened over time, creating a renewed tapestry of love.

62. BURNING HEARTBREAK SPELL

Intent: To release the pain of a past relationship, allowing emotional healing and the capacity to move forward with an open heart.

You Will Need:

- A black candle for absorbing negativity and sorrow
- A white candle for healing and new beginnings
- A piece of paper and a pen to write down feelings of heartbreak or memories you wish to let go of
- A fireproof bowl or cauldron
- Sage, rosemary, or other herbs associated with emotional healing and purification
- A piece of rose quartz to represent self-love and healing after the spell
- Salt to purify and protect your emotional well-being

Preparation:

1. Find a quiet space where you can perform the spell without interruptions, ideally a place where you feel safe and comfortable.

2. Cleanse the area and your items with sage smoke or your preferred method, setting a protective and healing space.

The Spell:

1. Light the black candle, and as it burns, visualize it absorbing all of your heartache and sorrow.
2. Write down the feelings of heartbreak or memories that you wish to release on the piece of paper.
3. Light the white candle, allowing its flame to represent the healing and light that is entering your life.
4. Sprinkle salt around both candles in a circle, creating a sacred space for your healing.
5. Carefully set the piece of paper on fire with the black candle, and place it in the fireproof bowl or cauldron to burn to ash, saying, "Pain of the past, I release you now, heal my heart, to this I vow."
6. As the paper burns, imagine the emotional ties to the past relationship dissolving with the smoke.
7. Hold the rose quartz, imbuing it with your desire for self-love and future happiness.

Sealing the Spell:

1. Extinguish the black candle, affirming that the pain has been absorbed and transformed.

2. Let the white candle burn down safely, or extinguish it as well, as a sign of your healing process beginning.

3. Dispose of the ashes by flushing them away, burying them outside, or allowing them to be carried off by a body of water, symbolizing your readiness to let go.

After the Spell:

1. Carry the rose quartz with you or place it under your pillow to encourage healing and self-love.

2. Engage in self-care practices, reinforcing the love and compassion you deserve.

3. Whenever you feel pangs of heartbreak, hold the rose quartz and remind yourself of your commitment to heal and move forward.

4. Reflect on the ritual and your feelings in the days that follow, noting any shifts in your emotional state or the beginning of closure.

The Burning Heartbreak Spell is a cathartic release, allowing you to consciously let go of past hurts and embrace the healing process with the support of symbolic ritual and the energies of transformative herbs and crystals.

63. MENDING HEARTBREAK TALISMAN

Intent: To create a personal talisman that will aid in the healing of a broken heart, providing comfort and encouraging emotional renewal.

You Will Need:

- A small cloth pouch or a square of fabric and ribbon
- A piece of rose quartz for its healing and heart-soothing properties
- Lavender buds for their calming and peaceful energy
- Chamomile for its association with relaxation and stress relief
- A small piece of paper and a pen to write down affirmations of self-love and healing
- A green candle to symbolize the heart chakra and emotional renewal
- Yarrow, known for its ability to heal emotional wounds
- A few drops of cypress or sandalwood oil for grounding and strength

Preparation:

1. Find a quiet space where you can concentrate on your healing intentions.

2. Cleanse the space, the pouch or fabric, and your talisman ingredients.

The Spell:

1. Light the green candle, focusing on the energy of the heart chakra opening and healing.

2. Write your affirmations of self-love and healing on the piece of paper. Fold it and place it in the pouch or at the center of the fabric.

3. Place the rose quartz over the affirmations, feeling its soothing vibrations.

4. Add lavender buds and chamomile to the pouch, allowing their calming scents to fill your senses.

5. Sprinkle yarrow into the mix, acknowledging its power to heal your heartache.

6. Anoint the contents with a few drops of cypress or sandalwood oil, invoking strength and emotional stability.

7. If using a square of fabric, gather the corners and tie them with a ribbon to create a pouch. If using a ready-made pouch, draw it closed.

Sealing the Spell:

1. Hold the completed talisman in your hands and say, "With each beat, my heart does mend, bringing heartache to an end."
2. Pass the talisman through the smoke of the candle or over the flame carefully, reaffirming your intention for healing.
3. Blow out the candle, visualizing your heart chakra glowing with renewed health and wholeness.

After the Spell:

1. Keep the talisman close to you, in your pocket, purse, or under your pillow, especially during moments when you feel the need for emotional support.
2. Touch it whenever you need reassurance, and repeat the affirmations to reinforce the healing process.
3. Occasionally open the talisman to reaffirm your intentions, replace herbs if needed, or to add new affirmations.
4. Consider carrying the talisman with you to places that may trigger emotional distress as a source of strength and comfort.

The Mending Heartbreak Talisman acts as a soothing balm for the soul, providing a constant source of support and a reminder of your inherent capacity for healing and love.

64. FIDELITY RING CHARM

Intent: To create a charm that promotes faithfulness and strengthens the commitment within a romantic relationship.

You Will Need:

- A small ring, which will serve as the physical representation of the charm
- A white candle for purity and truthfulness
- A piece of blue lace agate or lapis lazuli, stones that encourage honesty and open communication
- Rosemary, for remembrance and loyalty
- A small piece of paper and a pen to write your intention or affirmation
- Jasmine oil for love and prophetic dreams
- A square of blue cloth to wrap the ring, representing fidelity
- A length of silver thread or ribbon to tie the cloth

Preparation:

1. Find a quiet place where you can perform the spell without distractions.
2. Cleanse your space, the ring, and the other materials energetically to prepare them for the charm.

The Spell:

1. Light the white candle, and as you do, focus on the flame as a symbol of the enduring bond in your relationship.

2. Write your intention or affirmation for fidelity on the piece of paper. Fold it and place it beneath the candle.

3. Pass the ring through the candle's flame quickly (without damaging it or burning yourself), and say, "Ring of trust, ring of fire, fill my relationship with pure desire."

4. Anoint the ring with jasmine oil, imbuing it with the energy of love and commitment.

5. Place the ring on the blue cloth and set the blue lace agate or lapis lazuli stone on top of it. Sprinkle rosemary around it while speaking your intention for loyalty and faithfulness.

6. Fold the cloth around the ring and stone, forming a small bundle. Tie it with the silver thread or ribbon, saying, "With this knot, I seal our fate, to be true to each other, early or late."

Sealing the Spell:

1. Hold the charm in your hands, closing your eyes, and envisioning a strong, faithful bond between you and your partner.
2. Say, "May this charm ensure we stay true, in thought and deed, in all we do."
3. Let the candle burn down safely, solidifying your intention.

After the Spell:

1. Keep the ring charm in a place where both you and your partner frequent, or give it to your partner to wear or carry.
2. Occasionally anoint the charm with jasmine oil to refresh its power and reaffirm your intention.
3. Reflect on your relationship regularly, nurturing the trust and commitment you have built together.
4. Renew the charm annually, or as needed, to maintain its strength and relevance.

The Fidelity Ring Charm acts as a powerful symbol of loyalty and love, providing a constant reminder and energetic influence towards a faithful and committed romantic partnership.

65. LOVERS' BIND RUNE

Intent: To craft a bind rune that intertwines the runic symbols representing love, union, and harmony, aiming to strengthen a romantic relationship.

You Will Need:

- A piece of wood, stone, or paper to create your bind rune
- Red paint, ink, or a carving tool, depending on the material you're using for the bind rune
- The runes Gebo (ᚷ) for partnership and a gift, Wunjo (ᚹ) for joy and harmony, and Ehwaz (ᛖ) for trust and loyalty between partners
- A small dish of water to cleanse and consecrate your materials
- A pink or red candle for love and affection
- Rose petals to symbolize love
- A piece of paper and a pen to draft your bind rune design
- Lavender oil for calm and nurturing energy

Preparation:

1. Find a quiet space where you can work undisturbed on your bind rune.

2. Cleanse the area, your crafting materials, and yourself to ensure a sacred space for the creation of your talisman.

The Spell:

1. Light the pink or red candle, invoking the essence of love and warmth.

2. Sketch your bind rune on the piece of paper, combining Gebo, Wunjo, and Ehwaz in a design that feels harmonious and balanced to you.

3. Once satisfied with your design, recreate it on your chosen material—wood, stone, or paper—with red paint, ink, or by carving.

4. As you work on the bind rune, focus on your intention for a loving and harmonious relationship.

5. Sprinkle rose petals around the space where you are working, calling in the essence of romantic love.

6. Anoint the completed bind rune with lavender oil, and pass it over the flame of the candle (carefully, so as not to burn it or yourself) and through the rose petals, to consecrate it with the energy of your intention.

Sealing the Spell:

1. Hold the bind rune in your hands, close your eyes, and say, "Runes of old, bind our love true, bring harmony, joy, and trust anew."

2. Place the bind rune in front of the candle until the candle burns down, allowing the candle's energy to further charge the rune.

After the Spell:

1. Keep the bind rune in a shared space where you and your lover spend time together, or give it to them as a gift.

2. Whenever you see or touch the bind rune, remember the intention behind it and the love you share.

3. Refresh the bind rune's energy periodically by anointing it with lavender oil and placing it in the moonlight.

4. Use the bind rune as a meditation focus when you feel the need to reconnect with your partner on a deeper level.

The Lovers' Bind Rune acts as a visual and energetic symbol to deepen the connection between partners, drawing on ancient runic energies to foster love and harmony in a romantic relationship.

66. SWEETHEART SACHET

Intent: To craft a sachet that promotes feelings of love, romance, and emotional connection between you and your sweetheart.

You Will Need:

- A small pink or red cloth sachet or a square of fabric and a ribbon
- Dried rose petals to enhance feelings of love and romance
- Lavender for harmony and peaceful interactions
- Vanilla bean or a few drops of vanilla essence for sweetness and attraction
- A small rose quartz crystal for its loving energy
- A cinnamon stick for passion and to "heat up" affection
- A small piece of paper and a pen to write down your intentions or a love poem
- A few drops of jasmine or ylang-ylang oil for their sensual properties

Preparation:

1. Find a quiet space where you can focus on your intentions for love and romance.

2. Cleanse your space, the cloth, and your sachet ingredients energetically.

The Spell:

1. Lay out the pink or red cloth or open your sachet.

2. Write your intentions or a love poem on the small piece of paper. Fold it and place it inside the cloth or sachet.

3. Add the dried rose petals, invoking the essence of timeless romance.

4. Sprinkle lavender into the sachet, picturing harmonious and loving interactions with your sweetheart.

5. Place the vanilla bean or add a few drops of vanilla essence to the mix, intending to sweeten your relationship and enhance attraction.

6. Add the rose quartz crystal, affirming its role in providing loving energy and emotional connection.

7. Break the cinnamon stick into small pieces, or if it's already in pieces, add it to the sachet, visualizing your relationship filled with passion and desire.

8. Anoint the outside of the sachet with a few drops of jasmine or ylang-ylang oil, enhancing the love-drawing properties.

Sealing the Spell:

1. If using a cloth, gather the edges and tie them with a ribbon to form a pouch. If using a ready-made sachet, draw it closed.

2. Hold the completed sachet in your hands and say, "Sachet of love, sweet and true, strengthen the bond between me and you."

3. Keep the sachet under your pillow, in your drawer, or carry it with you to keep the romantic energy close.

After the Spell:

1. Whenever you are with your sweetheart, keep the sachet nearby to deepen the connection between you both.

2. Recharge the sachet by anointing it with the oil and placing it in the moonlight on nights of the full moon.

3. Periodically replace the ingredients to maintain the sachet's potency and reaffirm your intentions.

4. Reflect on the growth and sweetness in your relationship, acknowledging the sachet's influence in your romantic harmony.

The Sweetheart Sachet serves as a fragrant and tangible reminder of your love, carrying energies that foster romance and affectionate bonds.

67. ROSE PETAL MIST SPELL

Intent: To create a misting spray imbued with the essence of love, enhancing romantic feelings and self-love whenever used.

You Will Need:
- A clean spray bottle
- Distilled water as a base for your mist
- Fresh rose petals, preferably from red or pink roses, associated with love and passion
- A small piece of rose quartz to infuse the water with loving energy
- A few drops of rose essential oil for its strong connection to the heart
- A tablespoon of witch hazel or alcohol as a preservative and to blend the oil with water
- A pink or red candle to charge the mist with intent
- A piece of paper and a pen to write down your intentions for love

Preparation:
1. Find a peaceful space where you can prepare your mist without interruptions.

2. Cleanse the space, the spray bottle, and the ingredients energetically to ensure a pure and positive setting.

The Spell:

1. Light the pink or red candle, focusing on the flame as a beacon for attracting love and warmth.

2. Write your intentions for love on the piece of paper. Fold it and place it near the candle.

3. Fill the spray bottle with distilled water, leaving a little room at the top for the other ingredients.

4. Add the fresh rose petals to the water, visualizing each petal releasing its essence of love into the liquid.

5. Place the rose quartz in the bottle to charge the entire solution with vibrations of unconditional love.

6. Add a few drops of rose essential oil, picturing the mist enveloping you in a loving embrace with each spray.

7. Pour in the witch hazel or alcohol, which will help preserve the mist and keep the oil and water mixed.

8. Cap the bottle and gently shake it while saying, "Mist of rose, carry my plea, bring love and passion close to me."

Sealing the Spell:

1. Hold the bottle in your hands and visualize a pink light surrounding it, sealing the spell within.

2. Say, "With each spray, love's sweet scent, to attract and nurture love is meant."

3. Extinguish the candle safely, affirming the completion of your spell.

After the Spell:

1. Use the rose petal mist by spraying it around your aura, in your bedroom, or on your linens, inviting the essence of love into your space.

2. Recharge the bottle in the light of the full moon to maintain its potency.

3. Whenever you use the mist, focus on your intentions for love and let the fragrance remind you of the love you deserve and the love you wish to give.

4. Keep the intention paper in a safe place, such as your altar or a special box, as a physical representation of your spell.

The Rose Petal Mist Spell serves as a delightful way to surround yourself with the energies of love, using the enchanting power of roses to open the heart and encourage romance and self-appreciation.

68. SEVEN-DAY LOVE CANDLE SPELL

Intent: To perform a love-drawing spell over the course of seven days, building and releasing energy to attract a loving relationship into your life.

You Will Need:

- Seven pink candles for love and affection
- A plate or holder for the candles
- Rose oil for anointing the candles, associated with love
- Rose petals to represent the essence of romance
- A piece of paper and a pen to write your love intention or qualities you seek in a partner
- Vanilla pods or vanilla essence to sweeten the attraction
- A small rose quartz crystal to place on your altar or space to amplify love energies
- Lavender for calmness and emotional readiness

Preparation:

1. Choose a quiet place where you can carry out your ritual for seven consecutive days.

2. Cleanse the space, the candles, and all materials with sage smoke or your preferred method.

The Spell:

1. Write your love intention or desired qualities in a partner on the piece of paper. Place this under the candle holder or plate.
2. Anoint the first pink candle with rose oil, focusing on your intent for love.
3. Sprinkle rose petals around the base of the candle holder or plate.
4. Place the vanilla pods or add a few drops of vanilla essence near the candle, invoking sweetness in your future relationship.
5. Set the rose quartz crystal close to the candle to magnify the loving energy.
6. Sprinkle lavender around the crystal, inviting a peaceful and loving energy into your space.

The Ritual:

1. Each day, light a new pink candle, allowing it to burn safely while you focus on your intention for love.
2. Spend time visualizing the type of loving relationship you wish to attract, imagining the feelings and experiences you would like to have.

3. Repeat your love intention or read the qualities aloud as the candle burns.

4. Meditate on opening your heart and preparing yourself emotionally to welcome love into your life.

Sealing the Spell:

1. On the seventh day, after lighting the last candle, say, "By the seventh flame, I call to me a love that is true, so mote it be."

2. Allow the final candle to burn down completely, signifying the full release of your intent into the universe.

After the Spell:

1. Collect any remaining wax, rose petals, and the vanilla pods, and bury them in the earth as an offering to plant the seeds of your intention.

2. Keep the rose quartz crystal with you or place it in your bedroom to continue attracting love.

3. Reflect on your feelings of love and readiness each day, noting any changes in your journal.

4. Be open to the opportunities that come your way, and trust that the love you are meant to find is drawing closer.

The Seven-Day Love Candle Spell gradually builds the energy of attraction over the course of a week, culminating in a powerful statement of your openness to love and readiness for a fulfilling romantic relationship.

69. UNWANTED AFFECTION CHARM

Intent: To create a charm that gently repels unwanted romantic attention or affection, preserving your personal space and emotional well-being.

You Will Need:

- A small black pouch or a piece of black cloth and a ribbon to tie it
- A piece of hematite or black tourmaline for grounding and protective energy
- Dried nettle leaves for their protective properties
- Sage for cleansing and warding off unwanted energies
- A small piece of paper and a pen to write down your intent for personal boundaries
- A pinch of salt for purification and protection
- A white candle for clarity and positive energy

Preparation:

1. Find a quiet and private space where you can focus on your intent without distractions.

281 POWERFUL MAGIC SPELLS FOR BABY WITCHES

2. Cleanse your space and materials, creating a peaceful and protected area for the creation of your charm.

The Spell:

1. Light the white candle, focusing on the flame as a source of purity and positivity.

2. Write your intention on the small piece of paper, clearly stating your desire for personal boundaries and the repelling of unwanted affection. Fold it and place it inside the pouch or on the center of the cloth.

3. Place the hematite or black tourmaline in the pouch, envisioning a shield around you that blocks unwanted advances.

4. Add the dried nettle leaves, acknowledging their role in safeguarding your personal space.

5. Sprinkle the sage into the pouch, with the intent of cleansing away any unwelcome energies.

6. Add the pinch of salt, visualizing it absorbing negativity and reinforcing your boundaries.

7. If using a cloth, gather the edges and tie it with the ribbon to form a pouch. If using a ready-made pouch, draw it closed after all items are inside.

8. Hold the completed charm in your hands and say, "Charm of protection, charm of might, shield my heart and my aura bright."

Sealing the Spell:

1. Extinguish the candle, envisioning the smoke carrying away any residual energies of unwanted affection.
2. Place the charm under your pillow, in your purse, or carry it with you, especially in situations where you might encounter unwanted attention.

After the Spell:

1. Touch the charm whenever you feel the need to reinforce your emotional shields.
2. Regularly cleanse the charm by placing it in moonlight or smudging it with sage.
3. Reaffirm your intentions as needed, ensuring the charm remains potent and aligned with your personal energy.

The Unwanted Affection Charm is a discreet yet powerful way to maintain your emotional autonomy and comfort, creating an energetic barrier that honors your desire for only welcomed and consensual interactions.

70. CRYSTAL GRID FOR LOVE

Intent: To construct a crystal grid that amplifies and attracts loving energy, enhancing romance, self-love, and positive connections.

You Will Need:

- A cloth or board with a grid pattern, or you can freely arrange the crystals in a symmetrical pattern
- A central stone, such as a large rose quartz for love or a clear quartz point to amplify intentions
- Surrounding stones like rhodonite for emotional healing, pink tourmaline for compassion, and green aventurine for heart healing
- Small clear quartz points to direct energy towards the central stone or outwards to send love into your space
- A red or pink candle to symbolize love and affection
- Lavender or rose petals to sprinkle around your grid for peaceful and loving energy
- A piece of paper and a pen to write down your intentions for love

Preparation:

1. Find a quiet space where you can set up your grid and meditate on it undisturbed.

2. Cleanse the area and your crystals with smoke, sound, or your preferred method.

The Spell:

1. Write down your intentions for love on the piece of paper. Place it in the center of your grid area.

2. Set your central stone on top of your written intentions. If using a clear quartz point, direct the point upwards to send your intentions into the universe.

3. Begin placing your surrounding stones in a pattern that feels harmonious and balanced. As you place each stone, focus on the type of loving energy it represents and your desire for it in your life.

4. Point your clear quartz points towards the central stone to direct inward energy for personal love or outward to attract a romantic partner or enhance relationships around you.

5. Light the red or pink candle, and as you do, visualize your love life being illuminated with warmth and joy.

6. Sprinkle lavender or rose petals around your grid, calling in peace and loving vibrations.

Sealing the Spell:

1. Once your grid is complete, activate it by taking one of the quartz points and drawing an invisible line connecting all the stones, starting and ending at the central stone. As you do this, recite, "Stones of love, hear my plea, connect and bring love to me."

2. Place the candle nearby the grid, allowing it to burn down safely while focusing on the loving energy growing and filling the space.

After the Spell:

1. Sit with your grid daily, meditating on your intentions and feeling the loving energy.

2. Refresh the grid every month, especially under a full moon, to clean the stones and reset your intentions if needed.

3. Add new stones or elements to the grid as your intentions for love evolve or as you feel drawn to new aspects of love.

4. Keep the grid intact until you feel that your intentions have been manifested.

The Crystal Grid for Love serves as a powerful focal point for your desires, using the synergistic energies of the stones to attract and nurture the love that you seek or wish to deepen.

71. INVITING ROMANCE SPELL BOTTLE

Intent: To create a spell bottle that will act as a magnet for romance, drawing in passionate, joyful, and loving energies.

You Will Need:
- A small glass bottle with a cork or lid
- Red rose petals to attract passionate love
- Jasmine flowers for their association with romance and attraction
- Vanilla pods or a few drops of vanilla essence for sweetness in love
- Lavender buds for a calm and sincere approach to romance
- A small piece of paper and a pen to write your intentions or desires for romance
- A pink candle to symbolize affection and to seal the bottle
- Honey to sweeten your call for romance
- Cinnamon sticks for heating up passion

Preparation:
1. Find a quiet space where you can concentrate on your intentions for inviting romance into your life.

2. Cleanse your space, the bottle, and the ingredients energetically to ensure they are free from any previous energies.

The Spell:

1. Light the pink candle, setting the intention for warmth, love, and affection to fill your life.

2. Write your intentions or desires for romance on the small piece of paper. Fold it and place it inside the bottle.

3. Begin to layer the ingredients into the bottle—start with the red rose petals, then add the jasmine flowers, vanilla pods or essence, and lavender buds.

4. As you add each ingredient, focus on its romantic associations and your desire for romance.

5. Pour honey into the bottle, filling it up to about a third or half, to sweeten your life with the energy of love.

6. Add the cinnamon sticks to ignite the flame of passion within your future romantic encounters.

7. Once all the ingredients are inside, drip the pink candle wax over the cork or lid of the bottle to seal it, symbolizing the sealing of your intentions.

Sealing the Spell:

1. As the wax dries, hold the bottle and visualize your life blossoming with romance, filled with loving and passionate moments.

2. Say aloud, "Bottle of love, spell set tight, bring romance into the light."

3. Extinguish the candle, affirming the completion of your spell.

After the Spell:

1. Place the spell bottle somewhere in your home where you'll see it often, like your bedside table or a personal altar, to remind you of your intention.

2. Whenever you notice the bottle, imagine it drawing romantic opportunities towards you.

3. Open the bottle and refresh the ingredients every year, or when you feel the need to boost the spell's power.

4. Once you have found romance, open the bottle and thank the ingredients for their help. You can choose to bury them, release them into running water, or scatter them to the winds.

This Inviting Romance Spell Bottle serves as a beacon of love, filled with ingredients that carry your intention out into the universe to bring romance back into your life.

72. RELATIONSHIP POPPETS

Intent: To create two poppets that represent you and your partner, or potential partner, to strengthen your emotional bond and encourage a loving, healthy relationship.

You Will Need:

- Two pieces of cloth in colors that represent love and connection for you (common choices are pink for affection, red for passion, or green for growth)
- Stuffing material like cotton, herbs, or fabric scraps
- A red ribbon to tie the poppets together, symbolizing the connection
- Personal items from each person the poppets will represent (hair, small fabric pieces, etc.)
- Needle and thread for sewing the poppets
- Lavender for calm communication
- Rose petals for love and romance
- Basil for fidelity and mutual respect
- A small piece of rose quartz for each poppet to encourage unconditional love
- A taglock or symbol to represent each person in the relationship
- A pen and paper to write down intentions or affirmations

Preparation:

1. Find a quiet space where you can focus on the relationship and the qualities you wish to enhance or attract.

2. Cleanse your space, the materials, and the personal items to ensure pure intentions.

The Spell:

1. Cut the cloth into two humanoid shapes, large enough to hold the stuffing and personal items.

2. Write down your intentions or affirmations on the paper. Place them inside the corresponding poppets along with the personal items and rose quartz.

3. Begin to sew the poppets together, leaving an opening for stuffing.

4. As you stuff each poppet, mix in the lavender, rose petals, and basil, focusing on each herb's properties and your relationship intentions.

5. Once stuffed, sew the poppets closed, sealing your intentions inside.

6. Tie the poppets together with the red ribbon, affirming the bond between the two individuals they represent.

Sealing the Spell:

1. Hold the bound poppets and say, "With these poppets, I draw forth a bond of love, trust, and worth."

2. Place the poppets in a safe and respectful place, such as on an altar or in a shared space where both individuals spend time together.

After the Spell:

1. Occasionally anoint the poppets with lavender oil or rose water to refresh the loving energy.

2. Renew the ribbon binding the poppets during significant moments in the relationship, such as anniversaries.

3. Reflect on the relationship regularly, considering the growth and challenges faced, and adjust your intentions as needed.

4. If the relationship naturally ends or transforms, respectfully unbind and deconstruct the poppets, returning the materials to the earth.

Relationship Poppets serve as a physical representation of the connection between two people, focusing energy on nurturing and protecting the love shared.

73. SCRYING FOR LOVE

Intent: To use the divinatory method of scrying to gain insight into your love life, helping to reveal potential new love interests, the future of a current relationship, or guidance for emotional healing.

You Will Need:

- A reflective surface such as a scrying mirror, a bowl of water, or a crystal ball
- A quiet and dimly lit room to enhance focus and the scrying atmosphere
- A pink candle to symbolize love and to help set the mood
- Soft, instrumental music or silence, whichever best aids your concentration
- A journal or notepad and pen for recording any insights or images
- Rose petals to surround your scrying tool, inviting love into the session
- A comfortable seat or cushion to help you stay relaxed during the process

Preparation:

1. Arrange your scrying space in a quiet area where you won't be disturbed.

2. Place the pink candle and rose petals around your scrying tool.

3. If using water, you may choose to sprinkle a few rose petals in it as well.

4. Dim the lights or draw the curtains to create a conducive environment for scrying.

The Spell:

1. Light the pink candle, focusing on opening your heart to the insights you're about to receive.

2. Get comfortable and take a few deep breaths to relax and center yourself.

3. When you feel ready, gaze into your scrying tool, allowing your eyes to lose focus and your mind to open to whatever images, symbols, or feelings emerge.

4. Maintain a passive attitude, simply observing without actively trying to decipher what you see.

5. Stay open to any insights about love that come through, whether they relate to self-love, a current relationship, or a future love.

Sealing the Spell:

1. Once you feel the session is complete, take a moment to ground yourself by taking a few deep breaths, feeling the weight of your body in your seat, or having a glass of water.
2. Thank the universe, your subconscious, or any guides for the insights provided.
3. Snuff out the pink candle, symbolizing the closing of your scrying session.

After the Spell:

1. Write down everything you saw, felt, or thought during your scrying session in your journal. The act of writing may also help to clarify the meanings.
2. Reflect on these insights and how they may apply to your current situation or questions about love.
3. Pay attention to your dreams over the next few nights, as scrying can often continue to work through your subconscious.
4. If clarity about a specific issue wasn't achieved, consider repeating the scrying session after some days have passed.

Scrying for Love is a personal and introspective process, helping to reveal the depths of your heart and the potential paths your love life may take.

74. JEALOUSY MIRROR SPELL

Intent: To reflect and dissipate jealousy, either felt by you or directed towards you, promoting a sense of peace and self-assuredness.

You Will Need:

- A small mirror that can stand on its own
- A black candle for absorbing and neutralizing negative energy
- A white candle for purity and healing
- Salt for protection and cleansing
- A piece of paper and a pen to write down the feelings or instances of jealousy
- Sage or palo santo for smudging
- A clear quartz crystal to amplify clarity and protection
- A cloth to cover the mirror when not in use

Preparation:

1. Find a quiet space where you can focus on the spell without interruption.
2. Cleanse the area, the mirror, and other materials with sage or palo santo smoke.

The Spell:

1. Light the black candle, and as it burns, visualize it drawing in all the negative energy of jealousy.

2. Write down on the piece of paper the feelings of jealousy you're experiencing or the situations where you feel jealousy is being directed towards you.

3. Place the paper in front of the mirror, and then set the clear quartz crystal on top of it.

4. Sprinkle a circle of salt around the base of the mirror, creating a boundary for protection.

5. Light the white candle, and focus on it healing any hurt and purifying the energy around you.

6. Look into the mirror and say, "Mirror of reflection, mirror so bright, turn jealousy away, out of sight. Reflect it, deflect it, don't let it stay, I release these feelings, send them away."

7. Allow both candles to burn down safely. If you need to leave them, snuff them out—never leave burning candles unattended.

Sealing the Spell:

1. Once the candles have burned down, take the paper and burn it carefully in a fireproof container, signifying the release of jealousy.

2. Dispose of the salt by flushing it down the toilet or throwing it outside away from your home.
3. Cover the mirror with a cloth when you're not actively working with it to prevent reflecting and absorbing unwanted energies.

After the Spell:

1. Keep the clear quartz crystal with you or near the mirror to continue to absorb and transmute any feelings of jealousy.
2. Whenever you feel jealousy rising again, uncover the mirror and repeat the affirmation, visualizing the jealousy bouncing off the mirror and dissipating.
3. Cleanse the mirror regularly to ensure it doesn't hold onto negative energies.
4. Reflect on your feelings in a journal, noting any decrease in feelings of jealousy or the impact of others' jealousy on you.

This Jealousy Mirror Spell acts as a reflective shield, turning away the negative energy of jealousy and helping to cultivate a healthier, more positive outlook.

75. HEALING FULL MOON WATER

Intent: To harness the energy of the full moon to create water charged with healing properties, which can be used to promote emotional, physical, and spiritual well-being.

You Will Need:

- A clear glass jar or bottle with a lid
- Purified, spring, or distilled water to fill the jar
- A piece of clear quartz to amplify the healing energy of the moon
- A piece of amethyst for its healing and calming energies
- Moonstone if available, for its connection to the moon and emotional balance
- A small silver item or coin, as silver is associated with the moon's energy
- A label and a pen to mark your jar with your intention
- A white or silver ribbon to tie around the jar, symbolizing the lunar connection

Preparation:

1. Choose a location where you can safely leave the jar exposed to the full moonlight, such as a windowsill, balcony, or garden.

2. Cleanse your jar, the crystals, the silver item, and the space with sage smoke or your preferred cleansing method.

The Spell:

1. Fill the jar with your chosen water. If you are using tap water, you may want to let it sit for a day to allow any chlorine to evaporate before the ritual.

2. Place the clear quartz and amethyst inside the jar, and if you have moonstone, add that as well. These crystals should be cleansed and safe to place in water.

3. Drop the silver item or coin into the jar to imbue the water with lunar qualities.

4. Write your intention for healing on the label and fix it to the jar. You can also draw symbols associated with healing, such as the caduceus or ankh.

5. Tie the white or silver ribbon around the neck of the jar, setting the intention for it to act as a conductor for moon energy.

6. On the night of the full moon, place your jar in a spot where it can soak up the moon's rays, ideally leaving it overnight.

Sealing the Spell:

1. Once you place the jar under the full moon, say: "Moon above, so full and bright, charge this water with your light. Heal the body, mind, and soul, make my spirit whole and whole."

2. Leave the jar overnight to bask in the moon's glow.

After the Spell:

1. The following morning, retrieve your Healing Full Moon Water, and tie the ribbon to signify that the charging process is complete.

2. Store the water in a cool, dark place when not in use to preserve its energy.

3. Use the water in baths, as a drink (if you're sure it's safe and clean), in cooking, or to anoint yourself when you need healing energy.

4. Consider recharging the water each full moon to maintain or increase its potency.

This Healing Full Moon Water can serve as a versatile tool in various healing practices, from aiding meditation and ritual work to providing comfort during challenging times.

76. CLEANSING LIGHT SPELL

Intent: To cleanse your personal energy field or space of negative influences, creating a sanctuary of positive energy and light.

You Will Need:

- A white candle for purity and cleansing
- A clear quartz crystal to amplify energy and intention
- A small bowl of saltwater for purification
- Sage, rosemary, or cedar for smudging
- A bell or singing bowl for sound cleansing
- A piece of paper and a pen to write down any specific things you wish to cleanse from your aura or space
- Lavender or lemon essential oil for additional cleansing and to bring in positive energy

Preparation:

1. Find a time and place where you can perform the spell without interruptions.
2. Cleanse your space, the candle, and the other materials with the smoke from your chosen herb.

The Spell:

1. Light the white candle and set it in a central location within your space.

2. Write down on the piece of paper any negative energies, thoughts, or influences you wish to remove. Place it under the candle.

3. Hold the clear quartz crystal in your hand, and visualize it glowing with bright, cleansing light.

4. Sprinkle a few drops of the essential oil into the bowl of saltwater, swirling it gently with your fingers.

5. Dip your fingers into the saltwater and flick it lightly around your space, or anoint your forehead for personal cleansing, as you say, "Water and salt, cleanse and clear, remove all negativity from here."

6. Take the sage, rosemary, or cedar and smudge around your space, paying special attention to corners, doorways, and windows.

7. Ring the bell or play the singing bowl to send cleansing vibrations throughout the space.

8. Focus on the flame of the candle, imagining it filling the space with purifying light, and say, "Candle burn, bright and strong, cleanse my space, my mind, my song."

Sealing the Spell:

1. Sit quietly for a few moments, absorbing the peaceful and clean energy you've cultivated.
2. When you feel the process is complete, blow out the candle, visualizing the smoke carrying away the last remnants of negativity.
3. Dispose of the paper by burning it safely in the candle flame or burying it outside.

After the Spell:

1. Keep the clear quartz crystal near you or in the space as a continued cleanser and protector.
2. Whenever you feel the need for a quick energy cleanse, ring the bell, or spritz some of the saltwater around.
3. Repeat the spell monthly, or whenever you feel the energy in your space needs refreshing.
4. Maintain a clutter-free and clean environment to prevent the accumulation of stagnant energy.

The Cleansing Light Spell is a simple yet powerful way to maintain a serene environment, free from the residue of negativity and filled with light and positive energy.

77. HEALING BATH RITUAL

Intent: To create a ritual bath that harnesses the properties of water, herbs, and minerals to facilitate emotional and physical healing.

You Will Need:

- A bathtub filled with warm water
- Epsom salts for cleansing and to ease physical aches
- Lavender buds for relaxation and peace
- Chamomile flowers to soothe and calm the spirit
- Fresh rosemary sprigs for mental clarity and rejuvenation
- A few drops of eucalyptus oil for healing and to open airways
- A green candle to represent health and healing
- A clear quartz crystal to amplify healing intentions
- A cup of green tea or a bag of green tea leaves for antioxidant properties and to promote rejuvenation

Preparation:

1. Cleanse your bathroom to create a sacred space for your healing ritual.

2. Draw a bath with warm water, adjusting the temperature to your comfort level.

The Ritual:

1. Light the green candle near the bathtub, focusing on the intention of inviting health and healing into your space.

2. Add Epsom salts to the bath, stirring the water to help them dissolve while visualizing their purifying energy.

3. Sprinkle lavender buds, chamomile flowers, and rosemary sprigs into the water, releasing their healing properties.

4. Add a few drops of eucalyptus oil to the bath, breathing in the healing scent as it diffuses in the steam.

5. Place the clear quartz crystal at the edge of the bathtub or within the water to enhance and amplify the healing energies around you.

6. Steep the green tea in the bathwater, either by pouring in the cup of brewed tea or placing the tea bag directly into the bath.

Sealing the Ritual:

1. Step into the bath, immersing yourself in the water, and feel the warmth envelop you, carrying the healing energies of the herbs and oils.
2. Relax in the bath, meditating on healing light filling your body and spirit, repairing and rejuvenating every cell.
3. Stay in the bath until the water begins to cool, absorbing all the beneficial properties of the ingredients.
4. As you drain the tub, visualize any residual pain or negativity washing away down the drain.

After the Ritual:

1. Blow out the candle, affirming that your healing will continue even after the ritual has ended.
2. Drink a cup of green tea to continue the healing process from within.
3. Rest after the bath, allowing your body to recover and integrate the healing experience.
4. Cleanse the bathtub afterward to remove any residue from the herbs and oils.

This Healing Bath Ritual is a nurturing way to take time for yourself, promoting physical relaxation and emotional release, allowing healing on all levels.

78. RESTORING FLAME SPELL

Intent: To use the transformative power of fire to burn away old energies, habits, or situations, facilitating a period of renewal and restoration in your life.

You Will Need:

- A large fireproof bowl or cauldron
- A white candle for new beginnings and purification
- A red candle for vitality and renewal
- Strips of paper to write down what you wish to release or transform
- A pen to write your intentions
- Dried sage, cedar, or rosemary for smudging and purification
- A lighter or matches
- A piece of paper and a pen to write down your intentions for restoration
- Optional: essential oils such as peppermint or lemon for mental clarity and focus

Preparation:

1. Find a quiet space where you can perform the spell without interruptions.

2.   Cleanse your space and materials with the smoke from the dried herbs.

The Spell:

1.   Light the white candle, focusing on its pure flame as a symbol of the clean slate you wish to achieve.

2.   Write on the strips of paper the aspects of your life that you wish to burn away or transform.

3.   Light the red candle, envisioning the vibrant flame as the energy needed for your renewal.

4.   One by one, ignite the strips of paper from the red candle's flame, and carefully place them in the fireproof bowl to burn to ash, saying for each, "From flame to ash, from old to new, I release and transform you."

5.   As the paper burns, visualize the unwanted energies, habits, or situations dissolving and leaving room for new growth.

6.   Use the sage, cedar, or rosemary to smudge around the bowl and yourself, reinforcing the cleansing process.

Sealing the Spell:

1.   Write your intentions for what you wish to grow or restore in your life on the piece of paper.

2. Fold the paper and hold it over both candles (carefully), not to ignite it but to warm it, symbolically infusing it with the candles' energies.

3. Place the intention paper under the white candle.

4. Allow both candles to burn down safely, securing your intentions for restoration.

After the Spell:

1. Keep the intention paper in a safe place, like a personal altar, or carry it with you as a reminder of your commitment to renewal.

2. Take proactive steps towards the changes you wish to see manifest.

3. Reflect on the transformation process in your journal, noting any progress or new opportunities that arise.

4. When the intentions have been fully realized, burn the intention paper in a celebratory act of thanksgiving, or bury it to signify the full integration of the new energies into your life.

The Restoring Flame Spell uses the element of fire to symbolize the burning away of the old and the welcoming of rejuvenation and new beginnings.

79. HEAL YOUR SICKNESS WHILE YOU SLEEP SACHET

Intent: To craft a sachet filled with herbs and crystals that promote healing, designed to work with the body's natural restorative processes during sleep.

You Will Need:

- A small cloth bag or a piece of fabric and ribbon to create a sachet
- Dried eucalyptus for its health-promoting properties and to aid breathing
- Dried lavender to promote relaxation and restful sleep
- Chamomile flowers for their calming and anti-inflammatory effects
- Peppermint leaves to soothe and comfort the body
- A small piece of amethyst for its healing energy and to promote peaceful sleep
- A piece of clear quartz to amplify the healing intentions
- A small piece of paper and a pen to write down your intention for health

Preparation:

1. Find a peaceful time before bed to prepare your sachet.

2. Cleanse your space, the sachet materials, and the crystals.

The Spell:

1. Write your intention for healing on the piece of paper. Fold it and place it inside the sachet.

2. Add the dried eucalyptus, focusing on its cleansing and health-enhancing properties.

3. Include dried lavender, envisioning its scent lulling you into a deep, restorative sleep.

4. Place chamomile flowers into the sachet, feeling their warmth and healing energy.

5. Add peppermint leaves, imagining their coolness relieving any discomfort.

6. Place the amethyst and clear quartz crystals inside the sachet, setting your intention for them to work together to promote healing.

7. If using a piece of fabric, gather the edges and tie it with a ribbon to form a pouch. If using a ready-made sachet, draw it closed after all items are inside.

Sealing the Spell:

1. Hold the completed sachet in your hands, close your eyes, and quietly affirm, "With this sachet, I invite healing. May my body recover as I sleep, feeling refreshed and renewed upon waking."

After the Spell:

1. Place the sachet under your pillow or on your bedside table as you sleep.
2. Each night before you go to sleep, hold the sachet, reaffirming your intention for health and healing.
3. In the morning, give thanks for the healing that occurred during the night.
4. Refresh the contents of the sachet as needed, especially if you continue to feel unwell or as a way to maintain good health.

This Heal Your Sickness While You Sleep Sachet serves as a supportive tool, enhancing the body's natural healing process during the vital time of rest and sleep.

80. GROUNDING ANXIETY SPELL

Intent: To create a ritual that grounds your energy and calms anxious thoughts, bringing tranquility to your mind and spirit.

You Will Need:
- A brown or black candle for grounding and stability
- A small bowl of soil to symbolize the earth and its grounding properties
- A piece of paper and a pen to write down your anxious thoughts or worries
- Lavender or chamomile for calming the mind
- A grounding stone such as hematite, smoky quartz, or black tourmaline
- Essential oils such as vetiver, cedarwood, or sandalwood for grounding
- A white ribbon to tie your written anxieties, symbolizing clarity and peace

Preparation:
1. Find a quiet space where you can perform the spell without interruption.

2. Cleanse your space, the candle, and other materials with smoke or your chosen method.

The Spell:

1. Light the brown or black candle, envisioning its flame burning away the fog of anxiety.
2. Write down your anxieties on the piece of paper, pouring your worries onto the page.
3. Fold the paper and tie it with the white ribbon, then bury it in the bowl of soil, symbolizing the grounding of your thoughts.
4. Hold the lavender or chamomile in your hands, smelling its scent to help calm your senses.
5. Place the grounding stone in front of the candle, and anoint it with a drop of the essential oil. Hold it in your hands and feel its weight, allowing it to anchor you.
6. Sit with the candle and the stone, meditating on the sensation of being grounded. Visualize roots extending from your feet deep into the earth, stabilizing your energy.

Sealing the Spell:

1. Once you feel more centered, blow out the candle, imagining your anxiety being extinguished with the flame.

2. Keep the grounding stone with you, especially in situations where you know you might encounter stress.

After the Spell:

1. Whenever you feel anxiety creeping in, hold the grounding stone and remember the sensation of being rooted and stable.

2. At the end of each day, write down any anxious thoughts in a journal and then tear the page out. Tie it with the ribbon and bury it in the bowl of soil. This daily practice helps to continually ground and release anxiety.

3. Refresh the bowl of soil periodically, and consider planting something in it as a symbol of growth from your released anxieties.

The Grounding Anxiety Spell is designed to help you find calm in the present moment and to remind you that you have the power to control your inner landscape, even when external circumstances are challenging.

81. REBOOT POTION

Intent: To concoct a potion that helps to reset your mental state, providing clarity and renewed energy when you're feeling sluggish or mentally foggy.

You Will Need:

- A clear glass of purified or spring water as the base of your potion
- A slice of lemon for purification and mental clarity
- Fresh mint leaves for their refreshing and invigorating properties
- A sprig of rosemary for mental focus and memory
- A small piece of ginger for its energizing and warming effects
- Honey to sweeten the potion and add the energies of happiness and solar brightness
- A clear quartz crystal to amplify the potion's intentions
- A yellow or gold candle to represent renewed energy and vitality

Preparation:

1. Find a peaceful moment in your day to craft your potion, preferably in the morning or when you need a mental boost.

2. Cleanse your space and materials with your preferred method, ensuring that your potion will be made in a positive environment.

The Potion:

1. Light the yellow or gold candle, setting the intention for revitalization and renewed energy.
2. Pour the water into the glass, envisioning it as a vessel for clarity and refreshment.
3. Squeeze the lemon slice into the water, adding its cleansing properties and envisioning it cutting through mental fog.
4. Rub the mint leaves between your fingers to release their scent, and then place them in the water, imagining their crispness invigorating your mind.
5. Add the sprig of rosemary, focusing on its reputation for improving memory and concentration.
6. Grate a bit of ginger into the potion for an energetic spark, picturing it as a catalyst for your mental reboot.
7. Stir in a teaspoon of honey, infusing the potion with sweetness and light.
8. Place the clear quartz crystal near the glass or even into the water if it's safe to do so, to amplify and energize the potion's effects.

Sealing the Potion:

1. Hold the glass in both hands and say, "Potion of clarity, potion of might, refresh my mind, and restore my light."

2. Sit and meditate on the flame of the candle for a few moments, absorbing the feelings of renewal and awakening.

3. Extinguish the candle safely.

After the Potion:

1. Sip the potion slowly, savoring the flavors and imagining each sip brightening and energizing your mind.

2. Carry the clear quartz crystal with you throughout the day to maintain mental clarity.

3. Repeat the potion-making whenever you need a mental or energetic reboot, customizing the ingredients as your intuition guides you.

This Reboot Potion is a simple, natural way to give yourself a gentle, refreshing jolt back to mental alertness, aiding in overcoming moments of lethargy or mental fatigue.

82. CRYSTAL GRID FOR HEALING PAIN

Intent: To arrange a crystal grid with the purpose of alleviating physical pain and promoting the body's natural healing processes.

You Will Need:
- A cloth or board with a grid pattern, or you can freely arrange the crystals in a symmetrical pattern you're drawn to
- A central stone, such as a clear quartz point to amplify healing, or an amethyst for its pain-relieving properties
- Surrounding stones like malachite for its anti-inflammatory properties, bloodstone for circulation and healing, and blue lace agate for its soothing abilities
- Smaller clear quartz points to direct energy inward toward the central stone, enhancing the healing focus
- A green candle to represent health and healing
- Sage, cedar, or palo santo to cleanse the stones and your space

- A piece of paper and a pen to write your intention or a healing affirmation

Preparation:

1. Choose a location where your grid can remain undisturbed, such as on a bedside table or a healing space in your home.
2. Cleanse your chosen area and crystals with the smoke of sage, cedar, or palo santo.

The Spell:

1. Write your intention or healing affirmation on the piece of paper and place it at the center of your grid area.
2. Set your central stone over your written intention, visualizing it as the anchor for the healing energy.
3. Arrange your surrounding stones in the pattern on your grid, placing each stone with intention and focus on its healing properties.
4. Point the smaller clear quartz points toward the central stone, directing the flow of energy to enhance healing.
5. Light the green candle, seeing it as a symbol of the health and pain relief you are manifesting.

6. As you complete the setup, visualize the entire grid glowing with a healing light, pulsating with the potential to alleviate pain.

Sealing the Spell:

1. Once your grid is assembled, activate it by touching each stone with your finger or a crystal point, starting from the outer stones and moving towards the center, while saying, "Stones of healing, power unite, ease my pain, day and night."

2. Sit with the grid for a few moments, meditating on your intention and the relief you seek.

After the Spell:

1. Allow the green candle to burn down in a safe place while you're present, reinforcing the grid's healing intention.

2. Keep the grid intact, and spend time near it daily, focusing on your healing intention and visualizing the pain dissipating each time.

3. Recharge the grid under the light of the full moon to maintain its potency and cleanse the stones as needed.

4. Whenever you feel pain, hold your hands over the grid, drawing upon its energy, and visualize the pain being absorbed by the stones.

This Crystal Grid for Healing Pain serves as a touchstone for your healing journey, utilizing the combined energies of specific crystals known for their pain-relieving vibrations.

83. HEALING ENERGY POUCH

Intent: To assemble a pouch that you can carry with you, filled with items imbued with healing energies for both physical and emotional wellbeing.

You Will Need:

- A small cloth pouch, preferably in a soothing color like blue or green
- A piece of clear quartz to amplify healing intentions
- A piece of amethyst for its stress-relieving and healing properties
- A small piece of green aventurine for its ability to stimulate physical recovery
- Dried lavender for promoting relaxation and peace
- Dried chamomile flowers for their calming and soothing effects
- A small piece of paper and a pen to write a healing affirmation or intention
- A green or blue ribbon to tie the pouch, representing health and healing

Preparation:

1.   Find a peaceful time and space to focus on creating your healing energy pouch.

2.   Cleanse your space, the pouch, and the crystals with sage smoke or your preferred method.

The Spell:

1.   Write your healing affirmation or intention on the small piece of paper. Fold it and place it in the pouch.

2.   Place each crystal into the pouch, focusing on its healing properties and your intention for wellness as you do so.

3.   Add the dried lavender and chamomile, envisioning a sense of calm enveloping you.

4.   Once all items are in the pouch, draw it closed with the green or blue ribbon, tying three knots. With each knot, seal your intention by saying, "With this knot, I seal my intention for healing, may I be enveloped in wellness, may it be my shield."

5.   Hold the completed pouch in both hands and meditate briefly, visualizing a healing light surrounding you.

Sealing the Spell:

1. Keep the pouch with you as much as possible, especially during times when you feel in need of healing energy.

2. Whenever you touch or see the pouch, remember the healing intentions you've infused it with, and draw comfort from its presence.

After the Spell:

1. At the end of each day, hold the pouch and thank the elements inside for their support in your healing process.

2. If you're using the pouch to aid in healing from an illness or emotional upset, open it periodically to reaffirm your intention and replace herbs or affirmations as needed.

3. Once you feel healed, or when you wish to focus on a new area of healing, you can dismantle the pouch, cleanse the crystals for reuse, and return the herbs to the earth as a way of giving thanks.

The Healing Energy Pouch acts as a portable reservoir of soothing energies, providing support and comfort as you navigate through periods of healing.

84. PROTECTION SIGIL

Intent: To design a symbol that serves as a protective talisman, guarding against negative energies, harmful intentions, and psychic disturbances.

You Will Need:
- A piece of paper and a pen for creating the sigil
- A black marker or pen to finalize the sigil
- A small dish of salt for purification
- A white candle for purity and protection
- Sage, palo santo, or cedar for smudging
- Your personal item or representation (a lock of hair, a nail clipping, a photo, etc.) to link the sigil to your energy
- A piece of clear quartz or black tourmaline for reinforcing the sigil's protective properties
- An envelope or a small cloth pouch to carry the sigil with you

Preparation:
1. Find a calm and quiet space where you can concentrate on crafting your sigil.
2. Cleanse the area, the paper, and the other materials with the smoke of your chosen herb.

The Spell:

1. Light the white candle, focusing on the flame as a source of protective light.

2. Write down your intention for protection in a simple sentence on the piece of paper.

3. Draw out the letters of your intention, then begin to combine them into a single symbol or sigil. This should be a creative and intuitive process, allowing the sigil to form naturally as you focus on your intent.

4. Once you have a design you resonate with, redraw it with the black marker or pen, making it bold and clear.

5. Sprinkle salt over the sigil, or trace a circle of salt around it, saying, "Salt of the Earth, guard me from harm, protect me from negativity and disarm."

6. Pass the sigil through the sage, palo santo, or cedar smoke, and say, "Smoke of [sage/palo santo/cedar], cleanse this charm, let no psychic or emotional harm."

7. Place your personal item on the sigil to link it to your energy.

8. Set the clear quartz or black tourmaline on top of the sigil to charge it with protective power.

9. Fold the sigil around the stone and personal item, and place it in the envelope or cloth pouch.

Sealing the Spell:

1. Hold the envelope or pouch in your hands, close your eyes, and visualize a protective shield surrounding you.

2. Say, "By this sigil, I am shielded, by stone and smoke, my protection is sealed."

3. Keep the candle burning until it goes out on its own, or snuff it out if you must leave it unattended.

After the Spell:

1. Carry the sigil with you, especially in situations where you feel you need extra protection.

2. Place it under your pillow at night, in your car, or anywhere you wish to create a protective barrier.

3. Renew the sigil's power periodically, especially after challenging days or when you feel the need for a boost in protection.

4. When you feel the sigil has done its work, or if you wish to create a new one for a different purpose, cleanse the stone and dispose of the paper responsibly, returning it to the earth.

The Protection Sigil is a powerful, personalized talisman, crafted with intention to serve as a guardian against all forms of negativity that may cross your path.

85. IRON PROTECTION SPELL

Intent: To harness the historically protective properties of iron to create a shield against negative energies and malevolent forces.

You Will Need:

- An iron nail or object, as iron is traditionally believed to ward off evil
- A red cloth or ribbon to symbolize strength and protection
- A black candle for banishing negative energies
- Salt, for its purifying and protective properties
- A small bowl of water to represent cleansing and emotional clarity
- Sage or cedar for smudging and purification
- A piece of paper and a pen to write your protective intention

Preparation:

1. Find a quiet and safe space where you can set up your protection spell.
2. Cleanse the space and your materials using the sage or cedar smoke.

The Spell:

1. Light the black candle and focus on its flame being a beacon for protective energy.

2. Write your intention for protection on the piece of paper. Be specific about what you want to protect yourself from.

3. Wrap the piece of paper around the iron nail or object.

4. Tie the red cloth or ribbon around the paper-covered nail, binding your intention to the iron.

5. Pass the bound nail through the smoke of the sage or cedar, reinforcing the purification and protective energies.

6. Sprinkle salt into the bowl of water, and then dip the iron nail into it, visualizing the saltwater further cleansing and charging it with protective properties.

7. Say aloud, "Iron strong and fire bright, protect me with your might. Salt and water, cleanse and guard, against all harm, be my ward."

Sealing the Spell:

1. Place the iron nail in a safe place, such as near your front door, in your car, or carry it with you to ensure ongoing protection.

2. Let the black candle burn down safely, or snuff it out after you've completed your ritual if you need to leave it unattended.

After the Spell:

1. Whenever you feel the need for extra protection, hold the iron nail and remember the power you've imbued it with.

2. Renew the spell periodically, especially if you've been exposed to negative or harmful energies.

3. If you sense the iron nail has absorbed too much negativity over time, cleanse it in saltwater before recharging it with the black candle and smudging ritual.

The Iron Protection Spell leverages the old lore of iron's protective power, creating a talisman that acts as a guardian against negativity and harm.

86. FORGIVING SHOWER STEAMERS

Intent: To craft a set of shower steamers that release a blend of aromas designed to foster a sense of forgiveness and emotional release during your shower.

You Will Need:

- 1 cup of baking soda for cleansing and purifying
- 1/2 cup of citric acid for the fizzing reaction
- 1/2 cup of cornstarch to bind the ingredients
- 3 tablespoons of coconut oil for binding and nourishment
- Essential oils: rose for love and self-acceptance, frankincense for spiritual connection and grounding, and bergamot for uplifting the spirit and clearing away resentment
- A mold to shape your steamers, like an ice cube tray or silicone mold
- A bowl and spoon for mixing
- A spray bottle with water
- Optional: dried herbs like lavender or rose petals for extra calming properties and visual appeal

Preparation:

1. Find a time when you can focus on your intention of forgiveness without being disturbed.

2. Cleanse your space and materials, ensuring the energy is clear for creating your steamers.

The Spell:

1. In a bowl, mix the baking soda, citric acid, and cornstarch thoroughly.

2. Melt the coconut oil and stir it into the dry mixture.

3. Add a few drops of each essential oil: rose, frankincense, and bergamot. As you mix, focus on the intention behind each oil, inviting forgiveness and emotional healing.

4. Spritz the mixture with water from the spray bottle, just enough to get it to hold together without starting the fizzing reaction.

5. Press the mixture firmly into your molds, adding dried herbs if you choose to use them.

6. Leave the steamers to dry and harden for 24 hours in a cool, dry place.

Sealing the Spell:

1. Once the steamers are dry, unmold them, and hold one in your hands as you affirm, "With this steamer, I let go, allowing forgiveness to flow."

2.   Store the shower steamers in a dry place until you're
     ready to use them.

After the Spell:

1.   When you're ready for a shower, place a steamer on
     the shower floor where it will be splashed but not in
     the direct stream of water.

2.   As the steamer fizzes and releases its scents,
     visualize the steam carrying away any feelings of
     bitterness, resentment, or hurt.

3.   Let the warm water wash over you, imagining it
     rinsing away the last remnants of negative emotion,
     leaving you with a sense of peace and closure.

4.   After your shower, reflect on the act of forgiveness,
     whether you're forgiving yourself or someone else,
     and the space it creates for new beginnings.

Forgiving Shower Steamers offer a physical and aromatic
aid to the emotional process of forgiveness, helping to wash
away past hurts and open the heart to healing.

87. SHIELDING MIST

Intent: To produce a misting spray that can be used to create a barrier of protection around yourself or in your personal space, shielding from negative energies and influences.

You Will Need:
- A small, clean spray bottle
- Distilled or spring water to fill the bottle
- A few drops of black tourmaline essence or dissolved black tourmaline water for protection (ensure it's safe for spraying)
- Sage essential oil for cleansing and protection
- Cedarwood essential oil for grounding and strength
- A small clear quartz crystal to amplify the protective energies
- A white ribbon to tie around the bottle, symbolizing light and protection
- A piece of paper and a pen to write down your intention or a protective mantra

Preparation:
1. Find a calm space where you can focus on creating your shielding mist without distractions.

2. Cleanse your materials and space with sage smoke, if available, or by visualizing a bright light purifying the area and objects.

The Spell:

1. Fill the spray bottle with distilled or spring water as a pure base for your mist.
2. Add the black tourmaline essence or water to the bottle, focusing on its grounding and protective properties.
3. Drop in the sage and cedarwood essential oils while visualizing each droplet creating a stronger barrier against negativity.
4. Place the clear quartz crystal near or in front of the bottle to charge the mist with amplified intentions.
5. Write your intention or protective mantra on the paper. Fold it and place it underneath the bottle or tie it around the bottle with the white ribbon.
6. Hold the bottle in your hands and recite your intention or mantra, infusing the liquid with your energy and purpose.

Sealing the Spell:

1. Tie the white ribbon around the neck of the bottle as a final protective seal.

2. Say aloud, "With each spray, this mist will shield, in its protection, I am healed."

3. Store the mist in a cool, dark place when not in use to maintain its energetic integrity.

After the Spell:

1. Whenever you feel the need for extra protection, shake the bottle gently to reactivate the energies and spray the mist around your aura, workspace, or living area.

2. Reaffirm your protective intention with each use, visualizing an impenetrable shield forming around you.

3. Recharge the spray under the full moon or by placing the bottle on a windowsill in direct sunlight for a short period to "cleanse" the water inside.

4. If you used a quartz crystal to charge the mist, cleanse and recharge the crystal regularly to ensure it continues to amplify the protective energies effectively.

The Shielding Mist acts as a portable energetic guard, creating an immediate aura of safety and serenity whenever and wherever it is used.

88. PSYCHIC PROTECTION SHIELD

Intent: To create a protective barrier against psychic attacks, negative thoughts, and emotional vampirism, safeguarding your mental and emotional wellbeing.

You Will Need:

- A black candle for absorbing negativity
- A white candle for purity and positive energy
- A small piece of paper and a pen for writing protective affirmations
- Sage, palo santo, or cedar for smudging and clearing negative energies
- A piece of black tourmaline, obsidian, or amethyst for psychic protection
- Salt, preferably black or Himalayan, for grounding and protective boundaries
- A few drops of protective essential oils like frankincense, myrrh, or angelica
- A visualization of a protective shield or bubble around you

Preparation:

1. Choose a quiet place where you can perform the spell without interruption, ensuring your focus and energy are not scattered.

2. Cleanse your space and all materials with your chosen smudging herbs.

The Spell:

1. Light the black candle, envisioning its flame absorbing all negative psychic energy directed towards you.

2. Light the white candle, allowing its light to fill your space with positivity and protection.

3. Write down your protective affirmations on the piece of paper, focusing on strong, clear statements like, "I am surrounded by a shield of white light that only allows love and positive energy to penetrate."

4. Place the piece of protective crystal on top of the paper, reinforcing your intention with its energy.

5. Sprinkle salt around the base of the candles in a circle, creating a boundary that negative energy cannot cross.

6. Anoint the candles with a few drops of the protective essential oils, reinforcing the barrier against psychic attacks.

7. Close your eyes and visualize a bubble or shield of protective light surrounding you, strong and impenetrable.

Sealing the Spell:

1. Hold the protective crystal in your hand, and reaffirm your intention to be protected from all psychic harm.
2. Blow out the black candle, imagining it taking all absorbed negativity with it.
3. Let the white candle burn down safely, or snuff it out if you need to leave it unattended, while envisioning your protective shield solidifying around you.

After the Spell:

1. Carry the protective crystal with you as a personal talisman against psychic attacks.
2. Repeat the protective affirmations daily, especially before entering situations where you may feel vulnerable to psychic or emotional negativity.
3. Recharge your crystal regularly by placing it in sunlight or moonlight, and re-smudge your space as needed to maintain a clear and positive environment.

This Psychic Protection Shield spell is intended to fortify your spiritual defenses, creating a sanctuary for your mind and soul, free from the intrusions of unwanted psychic energy.

89. WARRIOR WITCH ANOINTING OIL

Intent: To concoct an anointing oil that imbues the wearer with strength, courage, and protection, enhancing their resolve and warding off negativity.

You Will Need:
- A base oil such as olive oil, almond oil, or jojoba oil
- Clove essential oil for protection and banishing negativity
- Rosemary essential oil for mental clarity and purification
- Black pepper essential oil for courage and protection
- A small dark glass bottle to mix and store the oil
- A piece of paper and a pen to write down your intention
- A small clear quartz crystal to amplify the protective energies
- A red candle to represent the warrior spirit

Preparation:
1. Find a quiet space where you can prepare your oil without interruptions.

2. Cleanse your space, the bottle, and the crystals using your preferred method.

The Spell:

1. Light the red candle, focusing on the flame as a source of strength and power.
2. Write your intention on the piece of paper. Fold it and place it near the candle.
3. Pour your base oil into the dark glass bottle until it is nearly full.
4. Add a few drops of each essential oil: clove, rosemary, and black pepper, while visualizing each drop adding a layer of strength and protection.
5. Hold the clear quartz crystal in your hand and charge it with your intention for the oil. Place it into the bottle with the oil.
6. Cap the bottle and roll it between your hands, warming the oil and blending the essences together.
7. As you do this, recite your intention or chant a mantra that resonates with the warrior spirit you wish to invoke.

Sealing the Spell:

1. Seal the bottle with wax from the red candle if desired, or simply screw the cap on tightly.

2. Say aloud, "With this oil, I anoint myself, a warrior witch with strength and stealth."

3. Extinguish the candle, envisioning your warrior spirit being locked into the oil.

After the Spell:

1. Anoint yourself with the oil before engaging in activities that require strength and courage.

2. Keep the oil in a cool, dark place when not in use to preserve its properties.

3. Recharge the oil under a full moon or by placing the bottle near the red candle during subsequent workings for added potency.

This Warrior Witch Anointing Oil serves as a powerful tool for those who wish to embody the attributes of a warrior, providing spiritual fortification and a boost to one's personal resolve.

90. CRYSTAL GRID FOR PROTECTION

Intent: To create a crystal grid aimed at providing a protective barrier against negative energies and harmful intentions, ensuring a safe and peaceful environment.

You Will Need:

- A central stone like a large black tourmaline for grounding and protection
- Surrounding stones such as smoky quartz for dissipating negativity, obsidian for psychic protection, and amethyst for creating a peaceful barrier
- Additional clear quartz points to direct and amplify the energy of the grid
- A cloth or board with a grid pattern, or you can arrange the crystals in a geometric pattern that resonates with protection for you
- A black candle for banishing and absorbing negativity
- Salt, to purify the space and create a boundary
- A piece of paper and a pen to write your intention for the grid

Preparation:

1. Choose a space where the grid can stay undisturbed, such as a corner of a room or a dedicated altar space.

2. Cleanse the area and your crystals with sage, palo santo, or by visualizing a bright light washing over them.

The Spell:

1. Write your protective intention on the piece of paper and place it in the center of your grid area.

2. Set the central stone, the black tourmaline, on top of your written intention, visualizing it as the anchor for your protective grid.

3. Arrange the smoky quartz, obsidian, and amethyst around the central stone in a way that feels intuitively protective to you.

4. Place the clear quartz points around the outer stones, pointing towards the central stone to direct the flow of energy inward, creating a strong protective field.

5. Light the black candle and set it near the grid, but not so close as to pose a danger. As it burns, see it absorbing all negative energy that comes against you.

6. Sprinkle a line of salt around the grid, envisioning it as a barrier that no negative influence can cross.

Sealing the Spell:

1. Once your grid is complete, activate it by touching each stone with your finger or a crystal point, starting from the outer stones and moving towards the center while reciting, "Stones of protection, strong and true, create a shield for me and you."

2. Visualize a bubble or dome of protective light emanating from the grid, enveloping your space.

After the Spell:

1. Leave the grid intact, and whenever you feel the need, reinforce its power by visualizing the protective dome and reciting your intention.

2. Allow the candle to burn down safely. If you need to leave, snuff out the candle and relight it when you return, until it's completely burned down.

3. Cleanse and recharge the stones periodically, especially after a heavy bout of negativity or if you've had many visitors to your space.

The Crystal Grid for Protection serves as an energetic fortification for your home or personal space, offering a constant source of security against all forms of negative energy.

91. STRENGTHENING YOUR SHIELD

Intent: To enhance your personal energy shield, reinforcing its capacity to deflect negativity and maintain your emotional and spiritual well-being.

You Will Need:
- A blue candle for calm and protective energy
- A piece of paper and a pen for writing down affirmations or intentions
- Protective herbs such as rosemary or sage, known for their shielding properties
- A selection of protective stones like black tourmaline, hematite, or smoky quartz
- A visualization of a strong, impenetrable shield or bubble around you
- A few drops of essential oils such as cedarwood or frankincense for grounding and strength
- A feather to represent the lightness and agility of your shield

Preparation:
1. Find a quiet space where you can concentrate without distractions.

2. Cleanse your area and materials with the smoke of the protective herbs.

The Spell:

1. Light the blue candle and focus on the flame as a source of protective energy.
2. Write your affirmations or intentions on the piece of paper, clearly defining the strength and impermeability of your shield.
3. Arrange the protective stones around the base of the candle, creating a circle of fortification.
4. Anoint the stones with a drop of the essential oil, reinforcing their ability to strengthen your shield.
5. Hold the feather and gently wave it over the candle flame and around the stones, symbolizing the light but strong nature of your shield.
6. Close your eyes and visualize a vibrant shield encircling you, glowing with the energy of the blue flame, the resilience of the stones, and the agility of the feather.

Sealing the Spell:

1. Repeat your affirmations or intentions, feeling the shield solidifying around you with each word.

2. Say aloud, "My shield is strong, my shield is clear, no negativity can come near."

3. Let the candle burn down safely, solidifying your protective work.

After the Spell:

1. Carry one of the protective stones with you as a reminder of your strengthened shield.

2. Whenever you enter a potentially negative environment, visualize your shield glowing brightly, repelling any harmful energies.

3. Revisit your affirmations regularly, especially during meditation or before sleep, to keep your shield robust.

4. Refresh the protective herbs and essential oil drops on your stones as needed to maintain their strength.

This Strengthening Your Shield spell is a proactive measure to reinforce your energetic boundaries, ensuring that your personal space remains a sanctuary of positivity and peace.

92. GOOD FORTUNE CHARM

Intent: To create a charm that attracts good luck, prosperity, and positive outcomes to the bearer.

You Will Need:

- A small green cloth or felt, as green is often associated with good fortune and abundance
- A ribbon or string to tie the charm
- A piece of citrine or green aventurine, crystals known for attracting wealth and good luck
- A cinnamon stick or a pinch of cinnamon powder for success and protection
- A few basil leaves for prosperity and good fortune
- A gold coin or a piece of pyrite (fool's gold) to represent wealth
- A bay leaf upon which you will write your wish for good fortune
- A white candle for purity and new beginnings

Preparation:

1. Find a quiet space where you can work on your charm undisturbed.

2. Cleanse the space and your materials with your preferred method, such as smudging with sage or palo santo.

The Spell:

1. Light the white candle to set a clear intention for luck and success.
2. Write your specific wish for good fortune on the bay leaf.
3. Lay out the green cloth and place the bay leaf in the center.
4. Place the citrine or green aventurine on top of the bay leaf, envisioning the crystal charging your wish with energy.
5. Add the cinnamon stick or sprinkle the cinnamon powder for success and protection.
6. Place the basil leaves to attract good fortune and the gold coin or pyrite to symbolize the wealth you wish to attract.
7. Gather the corners of the cloth and tie it with the ribbon or string, while saying, "Luck and fortune come to me, as I will, so it shall be."
8. Hold the charm in your hands, and visualize a bright light surrounding it, filling the charm with magnetic energy.

Sealing the Spell:

1. Snuff out the candle, symbolizing the locking in of your intent.

2. Keep the charm in your wallet, purse, or pocket, or place it in a space where you conduct financial matters.

After the Spell:

1. Touch the charm before engaging in activities related to your wish for good luck, reinforcing the connection to your intention.

2. Every full moon, place the charm in the moonlight to recharge its energies.

3. As you notice the positive effects of the charm, acknowledge them with gratitude, thus increasing its power.

This Good Fortune Charm acts as a beacon, drawing opportunities, prosperity, and success into the life of the one who possesses it.

93. SELF-ESTEEM TALISMAN

Intent: To create a talisman that serves as a constant source of positive energy and self-empowerment, enhancing self-esteem and confidence.

You Will Need:
- A small cloth pouch or a piece of fabric and string to make a pouch
- Sunstone, known for its properties of self-empowerment and independence
- Rose quartz, to promote self-love and emotional harmony
- Citrine, for its ability to boost confidence and self-expression
- Lavender or chamomile buds for calmness and reducing anxiety
- A small mirror or a shiny object to reflect your true self and reinforce positive self-image
- A piece of paper and a pen to write an affirmation of self-love and confidence
- A yellow or gold ribbon to tie the pouch, representing positivity and self-assurance

Preparation:

1. Choose a calm and private space to assemble your talisman.

2. Cleanse the area, the pouch, and the crystals with your preferred method.

The Spell:

1. Write your affirmation on the piece of paper. This could be something like, "I am worthy, I am confident, I am loved." Fold it and place it in the pouch.

2. Place each crystal into the pouch, focusing on their individual qualities and how they contribute to your self-esteem.

    *   Feel the warmth and power of the sunstone, igniting your inner strength.
    *   Hold the rose quartz, letting it fill you with self-love and acceptance.
    *   Grasp the citrine, envisioning it enhancing your confidence and self-expression.

3. Add lavender or chamomile buds to the pouch to promote calmness and reduce any feelings of anxiety.

4. Place the small mirror or shiny object in the pouch to remind you of your true worth and beauty.

5. Tie the pouch closed with the yellow or gold ribbon, sealing in the positive energies.

Sealing the Spell:

1. Hold the completed talisman in your hands and close your eyes. Visualize a warm, golden light surrounding you, filling you with confidence and self-worth.
2. Repeat your written affirmation aloud, affirming its truth and your belief in it.
3. Keep the talisman in a place where you will see and touch it daily, such as in your purse, on your desk, or by your bed.

After the Spell:

1. Whenever you feel in need of a boost in confidence or self-esteem, hold the talisman, repeat your affirmation, and draw strength from its energy.
2. Periodically, take the items out of the pouch, cleanse them, and recharge them with your intentions.
3. As your journey of self-love evolves, feel free to update your affirmation and add or replace items in the pouch as needed.

This Self-Esteem Talisman acts as a personal reminder of your worth and capabilities, helping to ground you in confidence and self-acceptance.

94. BODY COMFORT SPELL

Intent: To craft a spell that eases physical discomfort and aligns the body with energies of comfort and wellness.

You Will Need:
- A blue candle to represent healing and comfort
- Epsom salt or sea salt for its cleansing and soothing properties
- Lavender essential oil for relaxation and pain relief
- Chamomile flowers to reduce inflammation and promote serenity
- A small piece of paper and a pen to write a body-affirming intention or mantra
- A soft cloth or handkerchief
- A warm bath or a heat pack for its comforting warmth
- A piece of clear quartz or blue lace agate for their healing energies

Preparation:
1. Create a tranquil environment in a space where you can relax undisturbed, possibly near a bath if you choose to use one.

2. Cleanse your area and materials, perhaps with a few spritzes of lavender water or the smoke from a dried chamomile bundle.

The Spell:

1. Light the blue candle and focus on its flame as a source of soothing energy.

2. Write your intention or mantra for bodily comfort on the piece of paper. This could be as simple as "My body is at ease and free from discomfort."

3. Dissolve a handful of Epsom salt or sea salt in a warm bath or sprinkle it onto the heat pack, stating, "Salts of the Earth, absorb my pain, in water or warmth, let comfort reign."

4. Add a few drops of lavender essential oil to the bath or heat pack, and scatter the chamomile flowers, envisioning their properties seeping into your body, reducing pain and inflammation.

5. If using a bath, step into the water and soak, allowing the warmth to envelop you. If using a heat pack, apply it to the area of discomfort.

6. Hold the clear quartz or blue lace agate, and repeat your written intention or mantra, visualizing a wave of comfort cascading over your body.

Sealing the Spell:

1. Wrap the piece of paper around the stone and tie it within the soft cloth or handkerchief, creating a small pouch of comfort.
2. Extinguish the candle, visualizing the pain and discomfort being snuffed out along with the flame.

After the Spell:

1. Keep the small pouch with you, especially in times of physical discomfort, to remind you of the comfort you've invoked.
2. Renew the spell as needed, especially if experiencing chronic discomfort.
3. Take a moment each day to hold the stone, reinforcing your intention of bodily ease and freedom from pain.

The Body Comfort Spell is a gentle reminder of the body's innate ability to heal and find balance, supported by the nurturing energies of nature and intention.

95. INNER AMBITION SCRYING

Intent: To utilize the practice of scrying to reveal your deepest ambitions and the path to achieve them, clarifying your goals and the steps needed to realize them.

You Will Need:

- A reflective surface such as a scrying mirror, a dark bowl filled with water, or a crystal ball
- A quiet and dimly lit room to avoid distractions and enhance focus
- A purple candle to represent ambition, wisdom, and higher goals
- A notebook and pen for recording insights and reflections
- An amethyst crystal to enhance intuition and psychic abilities
- Sage, cedar, or palo santo for cleansing the scrying tool and space
- A comfortable seat or cushion to aid in relaxation during the scrying process

Preparation:

1. Select a location where you can be undisturbed, creating a serene atmosphere for scrying.
2. Cleanse your scrying tool and space with the smoke of your chosen herb to clear any residual energies.

The Spell:

1. Light the purple candle and set it beside your scrying tool, allowing its light to cast a soft glow.
2. Hold the amethyst crystal and set the intention to unlock your subconscious desires and ambitions.
3. Gaze into your scrying tool, letting your eyes relax and your mind open to the symbols and images that appear.
4. Stay receptive and patient, allowing the visions to come forth without forcing them or attempting immediate interpretation.
5. When you feel the scrying session is complete, or when images and insights begin to fade, gently bring yourself back to your surroundings.

Sealing the Spell:

1. Thank the elements and energies that have contributed to your session for their guidance.

2.   Snuff out the candle as a symbolic gesture of closing the session, preserving the insights gained.

3.   Write down any images, symbols, or feelings you experienced, even if they do not make sense initially.

After the Spell:

1.   Reflect on your scrying notes, researching symbols or images if necessary, to uncover the messages related to your ambitions.

2.   Keep the amethyst crystal with you as a touchstone to connect with your inner wisdom and to remind you of your scrying revelations.

3.   Repeat the scrying session periodically, especially when seeking direction or when at a crossroads with your ambitions.

Inner Ambition Scrying is a deeply personal and introspective practice, serving as a gateway to understanding your true aspirations and the ways in which you can achieve them.

96. SUCCESS OFFERING SPELL

Intent: To perform a ritual that honors and seeks the favor of energies or deities associated with success, creating an offering as a token of gratitude and a request for continued achievement and prosperity.

You Will Need:

- A gold or green candle to represent success and abundance
- A small plate or offering bowl
- Items to offer, which could include coins for financial success, a written statement of your goals, or natural offerings such as grains, fruit, or flowers
- Incense associated with prosperity, such as cinnamon, frankincense, or bayberry
- A small glass of water or wine to accompany the offering
- A piece of paper and a pen to write a letter of intent or prayer
- A clear quartz crystal to amplify your intentions
- A small bell to signal the beginning and end of the ritual

Preparation:

1. Find a quiet space where your ritual will be undisturbed.

2. Cleanse your space and materials with the incense, allowing the prosperity-associating scent to fill the area.

The Spell:

1. Light the gold or green candle, focusing on the flame as a beacon of success.

2. Arrange your offerings on the plate or bowl, and if using coins, you might choose to stack them or arrange them in a symbol of prosperity.

3. Pour the water or wine into the glass, placing it beside the offering plate as a symbol of hospitality and sharing.

4. Write your letter of intent or prayer, expressing your gratitude for past successes and your intentions for future goals.

5. Place the letter under the offering plate or bowl.

6. Set the clear quartz crystal near your offerings to enhance and broadcast your intentions.

7. Ring the bell once to signal the beginning of the ritual, then sit quietly, meditating on your successes and visualizing them multiplying.

8. Speak your letter of intent or prayer aloud, then fold it and leave it on the altar as part of your offerings.

Sealing the Spell:

1. Ring the bell again to signify the completion of the ritual.
2. Allow the candle to burn down safely, or snuff it out if you must leave it unattended.
3. Leave the offerings on your altar for a set period – this could be overnight, a full day, or until the candle burns out.
4. Dispose of the offerings in a respectful manner – burying them, leaving them in a natural place, or if appropriate, donating them.

After the Spell:

1. Take a moment to acknowledge any signs of success, however small, as affirmations that your offerings have been received.
2. Carry the clear quartz crystal with you or keep it in your workspace to maintain the connection to the energies of success.
3. Repeat the offering ritual periodically, especially at times when you are embarking on new ventures or seeking to boost your prosperity and achievements.

The Success Offering Spell is a powerful way to show appreciation for the success you've experienced while aligning your energy with the forces that can assist you in achieving further abundance and triumphs.

97. PLANTING HAPPINESS SPELL

Intent: To conduct a ritual that symbolizes planting seeds of happiness and joy, nurturing them to grow in your life, just as you would nurture a plant.

You Will Need:

- A small pot and some soil
- Seeds of a flowering plant known for its beauty and joyful energy, such as sunflowers or marigolds
- A yellow candle to represent happiness and positivity
- A piece of paper and a pen to write down your intentions for happiness
- Water for your plant, symbolizing nourishment for your intentions
- A small piece of citrine or sunstone, crystals that are associated with joy and positivity
- Optional: light, uplifting music to play during the ritual

Preparation:

1. Find a suitable space where your plant can grow, like a sunny windowsill.

2. Gather your materials and cleanse your space, the pot, the soil, and the seeds with your preferred method.

The Spell:

1. Light the yellow candle, and as it burns, focus on its bright energy infusing your space with happiness.

2. Write your intentions for happiness on the piece of paper. Fold it and place it at the bottom of the pot.

3. Fill the pot with soil, leaving enough room to plant your seeds.

4. Place the seeds in the soil, and as you cover them, visualize each seed representing a facet of happiness you wish to grow in your life.

5. Place the citrine or sunstone on top of the soil as a symbol of infusing your intentions with joy and positive energy.

6. Water the seeds gently, imagining this act as nurturing your happiness.

7. While the music plays, if you've chosen to use it, dance, sing, or simply move around the pot, infusing the space with dynamic and happy energy.

Sealing the Spell:

1. Blow out the candle, affirming, "As this flame extinguishes, my happiness grows."
2. Place the pot in a location where it will get enough sunlight, symbolizing the light that happiness brings.

After the Spell:

1. Regularly care for the plant by watering it, ensuring it has enough light, and removing any dead leaves or debris.
2. Each time you care for the plant, remember your intentions for happiness and visualize them growing and flourishing.
3. As the plant grows, take note of the happiness growing in your life, acknowledging and celebrating these moments.
4. Once the plant blooms, take time to appreciate its beauty and remember the journey you've been on to cultivate your own happiness.

The Planting Happiness Spell is a beautiful, living representation of the growth and nurturing of joy in your life, reminding you that happiness, like a plant, requires care and attention to flourish.

98. SUCCESS RUNE COOKIES

Intent: To bake cookies that are not only delicious but also imbued with symbols of success, using the power of runes to infuse each bite with positive energy for achieving goals and triumphs.

You Will Need:

- Your favorite cookie dough recipe (either homemade or store-bought)
- A toothpick or small knife to inscribe runes
- A baking sheet and parchment paper
- A symbol guide for runes, particularly those associated with success, such as Uruz (strength), Sowilo (success and solace), and Fehu (wealth and fulfillment)
- Optional: cinnamon or vanilla extract to add to the dough for their properties of attracting success and sweetening your endeavors

Preparation:

1. Preheat your oven according to your cookie recipe's instructions.

2. Prepare your cookie dough, optionally adding cinnamon or vanilla for their success-attracting properties.

The Spell:

1. Roll out your cookie dough and cut it into shapes large enough to inscribe runes onto.
2. As you cut each cookie, focus on your intentions for success and achievement.
3. Using the toothpick or small knife, carefully inscribe a rune onto each cookie. As you do this, say the name of the rune and a brief statement of its meaning. For example, while inscribing Uruz, you might say, "Uruz, rune of strength, empower my endeavors."
4. Place the inscribed cookies onto your baking sheet lined with parchment paper.
5. Before placing them in the oven, hold your hands over the cookies and visualize them glowing with a golden light, charging them with your intentions.

Baking the Cookies:

1. Bake the cookies according to your recipe's instructions.
2. As they bake, imagine the heat of the oven further energizing the runes and your intentions.

Sealing the Spell:

1. Once the cookies are baked and cooled, say, "With each bite, success I see, as I will it, so mote it be."

2. Store the cookies in a container where they will remain fresh.

After the Spell:

1. Eat a cookie when you need a boost of success energy, especially before important endeavors like meetings, interviews, or exams.

2. Share the cookies with friends, family, or colleagues, explaining the positive intentions (if you feel comfortable doing so) to spread the energy of success.

3. Remember to give thanks for the successes that come your way, recognizing the role of your intention and hard work in these achievements.

Success Rune Cookies serve as a delightful and tasty way to bring a touch of magic into your everyday life, combining the joy of baking with the powerful symbolism of runes for success.

99. BLANKET OF SECURITY SPELL

Intent: To infuse a blanket with protective energies, creating a physical and spiritual "blanket of security" that provides comfort and safety to whoever is enveloped by it.

You Will Need:

- A comfortable blanket, preferably in a soothing color like blue or green
- A white candle for purity and protection
- Lavender or chamomile essential oil for relaxation and peace
- A sprig of rosemary for mental clarity and protection
- A small piece of black tourmaline or obsidian for grounding and absorbing negativity
- A bowl of saltwater for purification
- A piece of paper and a pen to write down your protective intentions

Preparation:

1. Find a quiet space where you can lay out the blanket and work uninterrupted.
2. Cleanse your space and the blanket using the bowl of saltwater or your preferred cleansing method.

The Spell:

1. Light the white candle, focusing on the flame as a beacon of protective light.

2. Write your protective intentions on the piece of paper. Fold it and place it under the candle.

3. Anoint the corners of the blanket with a drop of lavender or chamomile essential oil, each time affirming your intention for protection and peace.

4. Lay the sprig of rosemary on the blanket, symbolizing mental clarity and an alert spirit against negativity.

5. Place the black tourmaline or obsidian on the blanket, charging it with the power to ground and absorb any harmful energies.

6. Gently wave the blanket over the candle flame (being extremely careful not to catch it on fire), allowing the light to symbolically infuse the fabric with protection.

Sealing the Spell:

1. Fold the blanket with the crystal and rosemary inside, and as you do, visualize it forming a protective barrier.

2. Say, "Blanket of security, woven tight, shield with warmth, day and night."

3.   Blow out the candle, symbolizing the setting and sealing of your intentions.

After the Spell:

1.   Use the blanket whenever you need an extra layer of comfort and security.
2.   Keep the blanket in a safe place when not in use, and recharge its energies periodically by repeating the anointing and intention-setting process.
3.   Cleanse the crystal and rosemary periodically, and replace them as needed to maintain the blanket's protective energies.

The Blanket of Security Spell transforms an ordinary blanket into a powerful tool of protection, offering physical and emotional comfort and safety to those who use it.

100. WITCH'S LADDER FOR SUCCESS AND ABUNDANCE

Intent: To create a Witch's Ladder, a powerful charm that uses symbolic knots and objects to attract and manifest success and abundance in your life.

You Will Need:

- A long cord or ribbon in a color symbolizing prosperity, such as green or gold
- Beads or small charms that represent different aspects of success and abundance
- Feathers or leaves, particularly those associated with prosperity (like bay leaves or oak leaves)
- Small coins or pieces of pyrite (fool's gold) to represent financial abundance
- A clear quartz crystal to amplify your intentions
- A piece of paper and a pen to write down your specific goals or affirmations
- A small bell to attach at the end of the ladder, signifying the calling of abundance

Preparation:

1. Find a quiet and comfortable space to work on your ladder.

2. Cleanse your space, the cord, and all materials with sage or incense to clear away any negative energy.

The Spell:

1. Write your specific goals or affirmations for success and abundance on the piece of paper. Fold it and place it near where you are working.

2. Tie a knot at one end of the cord or ribbon, symbolizing the start of your journey toward success.

3. As you add each bead, charm, or coin, focus on an aspect of abundance or success you wish to attract. With each addition, tie a knot and recite your goal or affirmation.

4. Intersperse feathers, leaves, and coins throughout the ladder. Each item adds its own energy, symbolizing different elements of prosperity and achievement.

5. Attach the clear quartz crystal to the ladder, infusing it with the power to amplify your intentions.

6. When you have finished, attach the bell to the end of the ladder as a symbol of clarity and to announce the arrival of abundance.

Sealing the Spell:

1. Once complete, hold your Witch's Ladder and visualize your goals manifesting. Imagine each knot and item glowing with potential.

2. Hang the ladder in your home, preferably in a place where you often work or meditate, to constantly attract the energy of abundance and success.

After the Spell:

1. Regularly touch and hold your ladder, especially when focusing on your goals, to reinforce its power and your intentions.

2. You can periodically add new items or affirmations to the ladder as your goals evolve or as you achieve them.

3. Celebrate and acknowledge any successes that come your way, big or small, as a sign of your ladder's influence in your life.

The Witch's Ladder for Success and Abundance is a dynamic and personal tool that serves as a daily reminder of your aspirations and the energies you are attracting to realize them.

101. UNITY KNOT SPELL

Intent: To create a powerful symbol of unity and connection, strengthening the bond between individuals, whether in a romantic relationship, friendship, or familial tie.

You Will Need:

- Two cords or ribbons, preferably in colors that represent the individuals involved (for example, each person's favorite color)
- A small white candle for purity and harmony
- Lavender or rose petals for love and peaceful interactions
- A clear quartz crystal to amplify unity and clarity in the relationship
- A small piece of paper and a pen to write down names or intentions for the relationship
- Optional: essential oils such as rose or ylang-ylang for love and harmony

Preparation:

1. Find a quiet space where you can perform the spell without interruptions.

2. Cleanse the space, the cords or ribbons, and other materials using the lavender or rose petals, or your preferred method.

The Spell:

1. Light the white candle, focusing on the intention of creating harmony and unity.
2. Write the names or intentions for the relationship on the piece of paper. Place it beneath the candle.
3. Lay the two cords or ribbons parallel to each other, representing the individuals in the relationship.
4. Begin braiding or knotting the cords together while focusing on your intentions for unity and understanding. With each knot or braid, recite your intention or a mantra that resonates with your goal.
5. Attach the clear quartz crystal to the knot or at the end of the braid, infusing the unity knot with its amplifying energy.
6. If using essential oils, anoint the knot with a drop or two, further enhancing the intention of harmony and connection.

Sealing the Spell:

1. Once the knot is complete, hold it between your hands and visualize a strong, unbreakable bond

forming between the individuals represented by the cords.

2. Say aloud, "This knot binds us in unity and love, blessed by the stars above."

3. Allow the candle to burn down safely, symbolizing the solidification of the bond.

After the Spell:

1. Keep the unity knot in a shared space, like a living area or bedroom, where both individuals spend time, to constantly reinforce the bond.

2. Occasionally hold the knot, especially during discussions or times together, to remind you of the unity and harmony you've created.

3. As your relationship grows and evolves, consider redoing the spell as a reaffirmation of your bond.

The Unity Knot Spell serves as a tangible representation of the strong connection between individuals, fostering harmony and deep understanding within the relationship.

CHAPTER 5.
SETTING UP YOUR
MAGICAL SPACE

Welcome to one of the most exciting aspects of your witchcraft journey—creating your very own magical space. This chapter is your guide to crafting a personal sanctuary where you can connect with your inner magic, perform the spells we've explored, and grow in your practice.

Whether you have a small corner in your room or a dedicated area in your home, this space will become a focal point for your magical workings. Remember those 101 spells we delved into earlier? This is where you'll bring them to life. Each spell, from the simplest to the more intricate, will benefit from being cast in a space that resonates with your energy and intention.

Creating a magical space isn't just about aesthetics; it's about making a place where your mind can quieten and your spirit can soar. It's a place of power, tranquility, and transformation. Here, surrounded by tools and symbols that hold personal meaning, you will tap into the deep well of power within you.

But what if you're a 'closet witch', someone who prefers to keep their practice discreet? Don't worry, this chapter has plenty of tips for you too. We'll explore how to create a portable or hidden altar and how to incorporate everyday objects in your practice to maintain privacy.

Your magical space is more than just a physical location. It's a sacred container for your hopes, dreams, and the rich tapestry of spells you will weave. It's where you'll celebrate your successes and learn from your experiences. Whether you're lighting a candle for a simple meditation or setting up for a complex ritual, this space will be a testament to your journey in witchcraft.

So, let's continue on this enchanting venture together, creating a space that is uniquely yours, where magic happens, and where every spell from our extensive collection can be woven with your personal touch.

CHOOSING YOUR SPACE

Welcome to the first and perhaps most crucial step in establishing your magical practice: choosing your space. This sanctuary, where you will commune with the elements, cast spells, and embark on your witchcraft journey, should be as special as the craft itself. Let's explore how to find the perfect spot in your home and, importantly, how nature can serve as an alternative or complement to your indoor space.

Finding Privacy in Your Sanctuary

Privacy is paramount in a magical space. It's where you can speak to the moon, whisper to the herbs, and chant your spells without the prying eyes of the world.

Start by exploring your living environment. Your sanctuary could be anywhere you feel a natural pull—a quiet corner of your bedroom, a less frequented part of your living room, or even a peaceful spot in your garden. The key is to find a place where you feel undisturbed and at peace, a spot that calls to you. Even a small area, like a window ledge that catches the morning sun or a cozy alcove, can become a powerful space for your magical workings.

Living with family, roommates, or in a bustling household might mean that finding an isolated spot is challenging. Here, creativity and adaptability are your allies. We go into detail on tips of 'closet witches' later in this chapter.

The Blessing of Natural Light
Wherever possible, let natural light infuse your sacred space. Sunlight brings vitality and clarity, empowering your spells and rituals. A spot near a window not only welcomes the sun's energy but also connects you with the moon's phases, an essential aspect for many spells.

A room with a window facing east captures the gentle morning light, ideal for rituals and spells that symbolize new beginnings or rejuvenation. Conversely, a west-facing window draws in the evening light, perfect for reflection and gratitude rituals.

Remember to align your spells with the sunrise or sunset to harness the specific energies these times of day offer. For instance, a sunrise spell can focus on awakening and clarity, while a sunset spell might revolve around letting go and peace

If your chosen space doesn't receive much natural light, there are ways to enhance what you have. Strategically placing mirrors can effectively amplify natural light. Position mirrors so they reflect the sunlight, brightening your space. Mirrors also symbolize clarity and truth, adding a deeper meaning to your practice. You can even consider using sun lamps that replicate natural sunlight. These can be particularly beneficial during winter or in regions with limited sunlight.

Embracing the Outdoors

Nature is a powerful ally in witchcraft. Practicing outdoors connects you directly with the elements, offering a sense of freedom and expansion. However, it also comes with challenges. Weather, privacy, and practicality of transporting your tools need consideration. For those who wish to blend indoor and outdoor practices, a portable altar can be a wonderful solution, allowing you to move your practice with the calling of your heart.

Whether indoors or out, your magical space is a reflection of your inner world. It's a sacred station where energies converge and where your craft takes physical form. Trust your instincts as you set up this space. Let it be a place that sings to your soul, a space where the spells from our extensive collection can be cast with power and purpose.

In choosing your space, listen to your intuition—it will often guide you to the perfect spot. Your chosen place, indoors or out, will become a sacred ground where your magical journey unfolds, grows, and thrives.

CREATING AN ALTAR

An altar is more than a physical space; it's a personal and spiritual epicenter where the material meets the mystical. It's a focal point for your energies, intentions, and the place where the spells from our collection will come to life. Here, you'll learn how to set up an altar that not only aligns with the basic tenets of witchcraft but also resonates deeply with your unique spiritual journey.

Essential Items for Your Altar

When setting up your altar, incorporating certain essential items can greatly enhance your practice. These elements serve as powerful tools and symbols, helping to focus your energies and intentions.

1. **Candles**: Integral to almost all magical practices, candles represent the fire element. They are not just sources of light but also focal points for meditation and intention setting. Use different colors to match the intent of your spells – red for passion, blue for healing, green for prosperity, and so on. The act of lighting a candle can be a ritual in itself, symbolizing the ignition of your will and desire.

2. **Crystals**: Each crystal possesses unique properties and energies. Select crystals that align with your current needs or intentions. For example, amethyst for spiritual growth, rose quartz for love, or citrine for abundance. Crystals can be placed on the altar to act as conduits and amplifiers of the energies you are working with.

3. **Symbols of the Elements**: Including representations of the four classical elements helps to balance your space. A bowl of water, a burning candle, a feather, or a small dish of sand or salt can each symbolize water, fire, air, and earth, respectively. These elements are the foundation of the natural world and can be called upon to lend their power to your workings.

4. **Representation of Deity or the Divine**: If your path includes deity work, incorporating a representation of a goddess, god, or any aspect of the divine can be a powerful addition to your altar. This could be in the form of a statue, a picture, or any symbol that you feel connected to. It serves as a reminder of the divine presence and your connection to it.

5. **Personal Sacred Items**: These are deeply personal and infuse your altar with your own energy. They could be family heirlooms, a gift from a loved one, or any object that holds special spiritual significance to you. These items make your altar uniquely yours and can serve as sources of strength and comfort during your practice.

Each item on your altar should be chosen with intention and placed with reverence, creating a sacred space that is a true reflection of your personal spiritual journey.

ARRANGING YOUR ALTAR

When arranging your altar, consider it a personal reflection of your spiritual journey. While there's no rigid way to do this, some guidelines can help create a harmonious space:

1. **Central Focus**: Choose a central item that holds
    special significance to you or your current work.
    This could be a symbol of your chosen deity, a
    representation of an element, or an item that
    resonates with your intention, like a crystal for clarity
    or a cauldron for transformation.

2. **Balance and Symmetry**: Aim for a visually and
    energetically balanced setup. If you place a candle
    on one side, consider balancing it with another
    candle or an object of similar size and energy on the
    opposite side. This symmetry helps in maintaining
    the flow of energy and creates a sense of harmony
    and order.

3. **Accessibility and Practicality**: Organize your altar
    so that the items you use most often are within easy
    reach. Avoid overcrowding; an overly cluttered altar
    can lead to chaotic energy and make your practice
    feel disorganized. Regularly reassess and rearrange
    your altar to suit your changing needs and the
    evolution of your practice.

4. **Personal Touch**: Finally, infuse your altar with
    personal touches. This could be photographs,
    heirlooms, or any item that holds deep personal

meaning and supports your magical intentions. Your altar is a sacred space, and personalizing it enhances the connection between you and your craft.

Personalizing Your Altar

Your altar should be a reflection of your unique path in witchcraft:

- **Seasonal Decorations**: For seasonal decorations, adorn your altar with items that reflect the current season or sabbat. In spring, fresh flowers symbolize growth and renewal; during autumn, leaves and acorns can represent harvest and gratitude. Aligning your altar with the Wheel of the Year not only honors the changing seasons but also keeps your practice in harmony with the natural rhythm of the earth.

- **Thematic Elements**: When focusing on a specific theme such as love or protection, add relevant items to your altar to reinforce your intention. For love, pink candles or rose quartz can create a harmonious atmosphere, while for protection, black stones like obsidian or protective symbols like an iron pentacle can fortify your space. These thematic elements serve as visual and energetic focal points, enhancing the power and focus of your spells.

- **Changing Layouts**: Absolutely, feel encouraged to adapt your altar's layout as your spiritual journey unfolds. As you explore different aspects of your practice or embark on new spells and rituals, rearranging your altar can reflect your growth and shifts in focus. This flexibility ensures that your sacred space remains a true reflection of your evolving path in witchcraft.

Maintenance and Respect

Maintaining and respecting your altar is crucial in keeping its energy vibrant and effective. Regularly cleanse your altar and its items to remove any stagnant or negative energy. You can use smudging techniques with sage or palo santo for a deep energetic cleanse. For a more gentle approach, lightly dusting your altar and its objects helps maintain a clean and respectful space. Periodically passing each item over a candle flame with intention also purifies and recharges them, reaffirming your connection and commitment to your magical practice. Remember, a well-cared-for altar is a powerful conduit for your spells and rituals.

Your altar is a sacred space where your spiritual practice is grounded. It's a place of power, creativity, and personal expression. As you arrange and personalize your altar, remember that it's a living part of your witchcraft journey, evolving just as you do on your magical path.

MAGICAL TOOLS AND THEIR CARE

For those beginning their journey into witchcraft, understanding and caring for your magical tools is key. These tools are not just instruments but symbolic representations of your intentions and energies. Here, we'll cover some essential tools and provide guidance on their maintenance.

Wands

- **Symbolism**: Wands are used to direct energy during rituals and spells. They symbolize the element of air and are often associated with communication and intuition.

- **Care**: To cleanse a wand, pass it through incense smoke or place it under moonlight. When not in use, store it in a cloth bag to protect its energy.

Athames

- **Symbolism**: An athame, or ritual knife, represents the element of fire. It's used to cast and dissolve circles, symbolizing the power to both create and dissolve barriers.

- **Care**: Athames should be cleansed by passing through flame or sunlight. It's important to handle your athame with respect and store it wrapped in cloth, separate from other tools.

Chalices

- **Symbolism**: The chalice represents the element of water and is often used to hold water or wine during rituals, symbolizing the essence of life and emotions.

- **Care**: Rinse your chalice with clear water after each use. For a deeper cleansing, fill it with saltwater and let it sit before rinsing. Store it in a place where it won't be used for mundane purposes.

Pentacles

- **Symbolism**: The pentacle, a five-pointed star within a circle, represents the element of earth. It's a symbol of protection and is often used to consecrate other tools or as a focal point during rituals.

- **Care**: Cleanse your pentacle by burying it in the earth overnight or smudging with sage. Store it in a velvet or natural cloth to maintain its energies.

General Care Tips for Magical Tools

Proper maintenance of your magical tools is essential to keep them charged and effective for your practice. Here's a look at general care tips:

Cleansing

- **Techniques**: Regular cleansing is vital to clear your tools of any residual or unwanted energies. Smudging with sage, palo santo, or incense is a popular method. You can also leave tools under the moonlight, especially during a full moon, for a deep energetic cleanse.

- **Using Natural Elements**: Earth and water can also be used for cleansing. Burying a tool in the earth allows it to discharge negative energy and recharge with natural vibrations. Similarly, running water can wash away negativity. However, be mindful of the material of your tools, as some may be damaged by water or prolonged burial.

- **Frequency**: Cleanse your tools regularly, especially after intense rituals or if they've been handled by others. A good practice is to cleanse them before and after each use to maintain their purity.

Consecration

- **Purpose**: Consecration sets your tools apart for sacred use. It involves cleansing them first and then performing a ritual to dedicate them to their magical purpose. This step is crucial in aligning the tool with your personal energy and intentions.

- **Ritual Process**: A simple consecration can involve holding the tool in your hands, visualizing it being filled with light, and stating its intended purpose aloud. You can also pass the tool through the elements— over a candle flame (fire), through incense smoke (air), sprinkled with water, and touched to a salt crystal (earth).

- **Personalization**: Feel free to add personal touches to your consecration ritual. This could include anointing the tool with a special oil, surrounding it with crystals, or reciting a personal chant or prayer.

Storage

- **Respecting the Tools**: Treat your tools with the same reverence you hold for your practice. They are not just objects but sacred instruments of your craft.

- **Proper Storage Methods**: Wrap your tools in natural fabrics like silk, cotton, or velvet. This protects their energy and prevents physical damage.

- **Designated Spaces**: If possible, store your tools in a special box or a designated area on your altar. For larger tools, like wands or athames, consider wall mounts or stands that respect their significance.

- **Accessibility and Order**: Arrange your storage in a way that keeps the tools accessible yet undisturbed. A well-organized storage system not only honors the tools but also makes your practice more fluid and intuitive.

Your magical tools are extensions of your intentions and energy. Taking care of them not only shows respect for the craft but also enhances your connection to these instruments of magic. Remember, each tool has its unique energy and purpose, and treating them with care will aid you significantly on your witchcraft journey.

CLEANSING AND PROTECTING YOUR SPACE

Ensuring your magical space is energetically cleansed and protected is crucial for your practice's integrity. Here's a brief yet comprehensive guide to maintaining a pure and secure magical environment.

Energetic Cleansing Methods:

Smudging: Use sage, palo santo, or sweetgrass to smudge your space. Light the herbs and gently waft the smoke around, paying special attention to corners and windows where energy can stagnate.

Sound Cleansing: Bells, chimes, or singing bowls can be used to break up stagnant energy through their vibrations. Move around your space with the sound, creating waves that cleanse the air.

Salt Water Sprinkling: Mix sea salt in water and sprinkle it in your space, or lightly dampen a cloth and wipe surfaces. Salt is known for its purifying properties and helps in neutralizing negative energies.

Creating Protective Barriers:

Visualization: Post-cleansing, close your eyes and visualize a barrier of light encircling your space. This acts as a shield, keeping the cleansed energy in and negative influences out.

Crystals for Protection: Place protective crystals like black tourmaline, obsidian, or selenite around your space. They not only act as guardians against negativity but also enhance the spiritual ambiance.

Use of Symbols or Sigils: Draw or place symbols of protection, like pentagrams or protective runes, at entry points to your space. These symbols serve as deterrents to negative energies and entities.

Maintaining Your Space:

Regular Cleansing: Incorporate these cleansing practices into your regular routine, ideally before and after major rituals or at least once a month.

Renewing Protective Measures: Recharge your protective crystals and reaffirm your protective visualizations and symbols periodically to maintain their strength.

By regularly cleansing and protecting your space, you create a stable and harmonious environment where your magical practice can flourish without interference.

CHAPTER 6.
PRACTICING IN SECRET: TIPS
FOR 'CLOSET WITCHES'

In the world of witchcraft, the path of a 'closet witch' is not uncommon. Whether you're embracing this journey out of personal preference or due to the environment around you, know that your practice is just as valid and powerful as any other. Keeping your craft discreet can be a unique and deeply personal experience. Here, we offer some practical advice to help you maintain your magical practice privately, ensuring your journey is both fulfilling and true to who you are.

Creating a Hidden or Portable Altar

For many practitioners who need to keep their witchcraft practice discreet, a hidden or portable altar is a perfect solution. These altars allow you to maintain a sacred space that blends seamlessly with your everyday environment or travels with you as needed.

- **Disguised Altars**: Look around your home for pieces of furniture that could double as an altar. A bookshelf with a dedicated shelf, a drawer in your dresser, or even a nightstand can serve as discreet altars. The key is to choose a spot that is part of your daily life but also holds a special significance for you.

  On your disguised altar, place items that are commonly found in a household but hold a personal spiritual significance. For example, a decorative bowl can hold crystals, a vase can be used for fresh herbs or flowers for your rituals, and a picture frame can hold images or symbols relevant to your practice.

One of the advantages of a disguised altar is the ease with which you can set it up and take it down. This allows you to perform your rituals when you have privacy and then return the space to its mundane appearance when needed.

- **Portable Altars**: A portable altar can be anything from a small wooden box to a fabric pouch, depending on your needs and the items you wish to include. The container should be easy to carry and discreet.

  Include small, easily transportable items that are essential for your practice. Miniature candles, small crystals, tiny vials for herbs or oils, a compact cloth to define your sacred space, and a small notebook or cards representing deities or symbols.

  Decorate your portable altar container in a way that resonates with you. This could be through painting, attaching charms, or sewing a pouch with fabrics that hold personal meaning.

Utilizing Everyday Items as Magical Tools

Incorporating everyday items into your witchcraft practice is not just a matter of convenience for those who must practice in secret; it's also a testament to the resourcefulness and creativity inherent in the craft. Here's how you can transform mundane items into potent magical tools.

Kitchen Witchery: Harnessing the Power

The art of kitchen witchery lies in transforming the ordinary into the magical, utilizing everyday items found in your kitchen as powerful tools in your craft. This approach is especially useful for those who practice discreetly, as it blends seamlessly into daily life

- **Transforming Utensils into Magical Tools**: Look at your kitchen with fresh eyes, seeing the potential in each utensil. A wooden spoon, for instance, can be much more than a stirring tool—it can direct energy and intentions, functioning as a wand. A regular pot takes on the role of a cauldron, a vessel where magical brews and potions are created, blending ingredients with intentions. Consider a simple strainer not just a tool to separate liquids from solids but as a symbol for filtering energies or sifting through ideas to find clarity.

- **Spices as Potent Herbal Correspondences**: Your spice rack can be a hidden arsenal of magical ingredients. Each spice holds specific properties that can be harnessed in your spells and rituals. Cinnamon, with its warm and protective properties, can be used in spells for protection or to add an energy boost. Basil, known for its associations with love and harmony, can be incorporated into love spells or used to create a peaceful home environment. Rosemary, a versatile herb, is perfect for purification rituals, memory enhancement, or even to foster loyalty. These common kitchen spices, often overlooked, are as powerful as any traditionally used herb in witchcraft.

- **Cooking as a Form of Ritual**: Embrace the act of cooking as a magical ritual. As you chop, stir, and simmer, do so with intention. Cooking then becomes an act of spellcasting, where each ingredient is added not just for flavor but for the specific energies it brings to the dish. Whether you're preparing a meal for health, prosperity, love, or protection, infuse each action with your desired outcome, turning a mundane task into a powerful magical act.

Nature's Gifts: Embracing the Magic Around You

The natural world offers a plethora of tools that are readily available and carry potent magical energies. These elements, often overlooked, can be central to a witch's practice, especially when discretion is key.

- **Stones, Leaves, and Flowers as Magical Tools**: Every natural element holds its unique energy that can be harnessed in witchcraft. Smooth stones, found during a walk or in your backyard, can be charged with your intentions and used in a variety of spells. They can be placed on your altar, carried with you, or used as focal points during meditation. Leaves and flowers, each with their distinct magical properties, can be gathered from your garden or a local park. For example, oak leaves can be used for strength, daisies for innocence and simplicity, and roses for love and passion. These elements can be used in spell jars, as offerings, or simply placed on your altar to draw their energies into your space.

- **Creating a Natural Altar**: Utilizing these natural elements, you can create an altar that is not only effective but also blends seamlessly with your environment. A windowsill that catches the morning sun or a small table in a quiet corner of your home can be transformed into a sacred space. Arrange stones, leaves, and flowers on this surface in a way that aligns with your current intentions, follows the natural rhythm of the seasons, or simply appeals to your sense of beauty and harmony. This altar can be as dynamic as nature itself, changing with your needs, the seasons, and the materials you have at hand.

- **The Art of Disguise**: One of the most significant advantages of using natural elements in your practice is their ability to remain inconspicuous. To the uninitiated, your collection of stones, leaves, and flowers is simply a beautiful, natural decoration. But for you, each element is a chosen tool, imbued with specific energies and intent. This allows you to practice openly, drawing on the power of these elements without revealing the true extent of your craft to those around you.

Reclaiming and Repurposing

In the craft of witchcraft, there is a unique beauty in reclaiming and repurposing everyday items for magical use. This practice not only connects you to the objects in your environment but also encourages a sustainable approach to your craft. Start by taking a look around your home with a fresh perspective. Items that may seem mundane at first glance can be transformed into powerful tools of magic. For instance, an old scarf, with its textures and patterns, might be reborn as an altar cloth, adding a personal touch to your sacred space. Vintage jars, with their history and character, can become vessels for holding moon water or storing herbs. Family heirlooms hold a particularly special energy; they can act as physical representations of your lineage or ancestral energies, connecting you to your past and the energies that have shaped you.

The key to repurposing lies in the intent you infuse into these items. It's a process of seeing beyond their conventional use and recognizing their potential in your magical practice. A simple cup, for example, can be transformed into a chalice to hold sacred water, imbued with your intentions during rituals. A picture frame might be used to create a focus for your intention, encasing sigils, symbols, or images that resonate with your magical goals. Even items like nails, stones picked up from a walk, or feathers found on a hike can become talismans or protective charms, depending on how you consecrate and employ them in your practice.

Moreover, this approach to witchcraft encourages a deeper connection between your spiritual practice and your everyday life. By finding the magic in common items, you're reminded that the sacred is not separate from the world around you but intertwined with your daily experiences. This realization can deepen your practice, making it more integrated and accessible. Repurposing items with intention is a powerful reminder that magic is everywhere and in everything, waiting to be acknowledged and harnessed. It's a practice that fosters creativity, resourcefulness, and a profound sense of connection to the objects that make up your world.

PRACTICING WITHOUT DRAWING ATTENTION

For those who need to keep their witchcraft practice discreet, there are effective ways to perform spells and rituals without drawing attention. These methods ensure that your practice remains personal and private, yet still powerful.

Silent Spells: The Power of the Mind

In witchcraft, harnessing the power of the mind can be particularly essential for those practicing discreetly. Silent spells offer an introspective and potent avenue for spellcasting, allowing practitioners to focus their intentions without the need for spoken words. Utilizing meditation and visualization techniques, these spells involve creating detailed mental imagery of the desired outcome. This form of spellcasting isn't just about picturing the end result; it involves immersing yourself in the emotions and sensations associated with achieving your goals. By vividly imagining these outcomes, you're able to channel your energy and intent directly into the fabric of reality, making silent spells a deeply personal and often very powerful form of magic.

Another method of silent spellcasting is through the written word. Writing down your spells and intentions can be a meditative and intentional act. As you transfer your thoughts to paper, you're effectively imbuing them with your energy. Once written, these intentions can be kept in a safe place, such as your altar, allowing them to continuously soak in your energy. Alternatively, for a more immediate release, you can burn the paper as a way of sending your intentions out into the universe. This act of burning not only signifies the release of your desires but also serves as a physical manifestation of your commitment to your goals, all while maintaining the privacy of your practice.

Gesture-based rituals represent another facet of silent spellcasting. These involve using specific hand movements, drawing sigils in the air, or arranging items in meaningful patterns as a way to direct energy and signify intentions.

Such gestures can be subtle enough to be integrated into your daily life, allowing you to perform magical workings almost anywhere without drawing attention. This method connects the physical with the spiritual, grounding your intentions in the physical world while keeping your practice personal and discreet.

Digital Grimoires: Embracing Modern Witchcraft

In an era where digital technology has become a part of our everyday lives, it offers a unique and modern approach to practicing witchcraft, especially for those who prefer to keep their craft discreet. Keeping your Book of Shadows or grimoire in a digital format serves multiple purposes – it ensures privacy and brings unparalleled convenience. By using password-protected files or specialized apps designed for magical practices, you can securely store your spells, notes, and experiences away from prying eyes. This digital approach opens up a world of resources right at your fingertips. The internet is rich with e-books covering various aspects of witchcraft, expansive online libraries, and even digital copies of ancient texts. Many found on The Lost Book Project. Incorporating these into your study and practice not only broadens your knowledge base but also allows for discreet research and learning, an invaluable asset for the modern witch navigating a private practice.

The organizational benefits of a digital grimoire cannot be overstated. Unlike traditional paper books, digital files offer the flexibility of easy organization and editing. You can effortlessly categorize your spells, rituals, and reflections; add images, links, and even audio that resonate with your practice; and make updates as your craft evolves. This dynamic nature of a digital grimoire means it can grow and change with you, reflecting your journey in the craft in real-time. Additionally, regular backups to cloud storage or an external drive safeguard your valuable magical insights and experiences. This practice not only protects against technical issues but also ensures that your wealth of knowledge is accessible across various devices, making it possible to carry your magical library with you wherever you go. In essence, a digital grimoire is not just a tool for secrecy but a modern companion that aligns with the evolving nature of witchcraft in our contemporary world.

Respecting Your Comfort Level

Embracing your unique journey in witchcraft means respecting and accepting your comfort level with how open you are about your practice. It's crucial to recognize that every witch's path is deeply personal and varies greatly. Some may find solace and power in sharing their craft with the world, while others may derive the same from the quiet, solitary confines of their private practice. Both approaches are equally valid and potent. The key is in understanding and honoring what feels right for you. Self-acceptance is a significant part of this journey. It involves acknowledging that your way of practicing witchcraft – whether out in the open or behind closed doors – is a reflection of your individual needs, beliefs, and circumstances. It's about finding comfort in your chosen path and owning it with confidence and pride.

In today's interconnected world, finding a community that resonates with your approach to witchcraft can greatly enhance your journey, even if you prefer to keep your practice private. Online communities offer a unique space where you can connect with like-minded individuals while maintaining your anonymity. These digital havens allow you to share experiences, seek advice, and learn from others without the need to reveal your identity. They can be a source of support, inspiration, and wisdom, helping you feel connected to the broader witchcraft community while still respecting your personal boundaries. Engaging with these communities can be a comforting reminder that, though your practice may be private, you are not alone on your path.

Practicing witchcraft discreetly is not just a matter of necessity for some, but it can also become a uniquely intimate and personal aspect of your journey. With creativity and a touch of ingenuity, you can cultivate a practice that is both private and potent. Whether it's through the quiet power of meditation, the subtle language of gestures, or the modern approach of digital tools, your craft can flourish in its own special way. This path underscores a fundamental truth of witchcraft: the true essence of your magic is rooted in your intentions and inner strength, far beyond the need for outward display. Embrace this path with confidence, knowing that your discreet practice is a profound testament to the adaptability and depth of the craft.

CHAPTER 7.
THE SAFETY OF
SPELLWORK

Embarking on the path of witchcraft is an exciting and transformative journey, one that opens up a world of possibilities and personal growth. However, as with any powerful practice, it comes with its own set of responsibilities and considerations. This chapter is dedicated to understanding the crucial aspects of safety and ethics within witchcraft, serving as a foundational guide for both beginners and seasoned practitioners.

The realm of witchcraft, filled with diverse practices and beliefs, is not just about casting spells or performing rituals; it's also about understanding and respecting the forces we engage with. Safety in witchcraft extends beyond the physical; it encompasses your mental, emotional, and spiritual well-being. As a practitioner, it's essential to approach your craft with a sense of responsibility, not only for your own safety but also for the impact your practice has on others and the world around you.

Ethics in witchcraft is a subject of deep importance. It involves recognizing the boundaries and consent of others, understanding the consequences of your magical work, and being mindful of the intentions behind your spells and rituals. Concepts like the Wiccan Rede and the Law of Threefold

Return are not merely guidelines but pivotal principles that underline the moral fiber of many magical practices.

As we delve deeper into the aspects of safety and ethics, remember that witchcraft is a deeply personal journey, one that requires introspection, understanding, and a commitment to practicing harmlessly and respectfully. This chapter aims to equip you with the knowledge and tools to navigate your path safely, ensuring that your journey into witchcraft is not only fulfilling but also grounded in a strong ethical framework.

SPIRITUAL SAFETY:
SHIELDING, GROUNDING, AND CLEANSING

In the practice of witchcraft, spiritual safety is paramount. This involves protecting yourself from negative energies, maintaining your energetic balance, and regularly cleansing your spiritual space. Understanding and practicing these techniques is crucial for a harmonious and safe witchcraft journey.

Techniques for Effective Spiritual Shielding

- **Creating Energy Shields**: Creating energy shields is a vital practice in witchcraft for maintaining spiritual safety. This technique involves the visualization of a protective barrier around oneself, commonly imagined as a sphere of light or a bubble that envelops your entire being. The purpose of this shield is to act as a filter—blocking negative or harmful energies from entering your personal space while allowing positive, nurturing energies to pass through. The effectiveness of an energy shield largely depends on the strength of your visualization and intention.

To reinforce your energy shield, regular practice is key. Dedicate time each day for visualization exercises where you focus on building and maintaining your shield. Picture it in vivid detail—its color, texture, and the sensation of safety it provides. Feel the shield solidifying around you, becoming a tangible force of protection. Alongside visualization, affirmations can be powerful in strengthening your shield. Phrases like "I am surrounded by protection" or "My energy is safe and secure" can be repeated to fortify the intention behind your shield

- **Using Protective Sigils**: Sigils are a fundamental aspect of many magical practices, serving as powerful symbols imbued with specific intentions.

Particularly in the realm of protection, sigils act as potent guardians and enhancers of energetic boundaries. They are not just symbols; they are visual spells, each line and curve charged with meaning and purpose.

The process of creating a sigil often starts with an intention, like "I am protected from negative energies." This intention is then broken down into its core letters and artistically combined into a unique symbol. The act of designing your sigil is a meditative process, where you infuse the symbol with your energy and intent.

Throughout history, various cultures have used sigils for protection. The Pentagram, for instance, is a well-known symbol of protection in Wiccan and Neopagan traditions. The Helm of Awe, a symbol from Norse mythology, was used by warriors for protection and invincibility. The Eye of Horus from Egyptian symbolism is another ancient sigil, believed to provide safety and health.

Once you've created your sigil, it needs to be charged or activated. This can be done through focused meditation, visualizing the sigil glowing with energy, or by passing it through the smoke of a cleansing herb like sage. Some practitioners use moonlight or sunlight to charge their sigils, while others might bury them in the earth for a night.

Grounding Practices to Maintain Balance

Grounding practices are essential in witchcraft for maintaining energetic balance and stability, especially after engaging in intense magical work. These practices help in reconnecting with the earth's energy, discharging any excess energy, and centering yourself.

One effective grounding method is connecting with nature. Nature, with its inherent grounding properties, provides a natural way to release excess energies and realign your own. Spending time outdoors, engaging in simple acts like walking barefoot on the grass or soil, allows you to directly connect with the earth's stabilizing energy. The act of grounding doesn't need to be complex; it can be as simple as touching plants, hugging a tree, or just sitting quietly in a natural setting. These activities enable you to tune into the natural rhythms of the earth, helping to bring your own energy into balance.

Visualization and meditation are also powerful grounding tools. A common grounding technique involves visualizing roots growing from the soles of your feet or the base of your spine, extending deep into the earth. As you visualize these roots, imagine them anchoring you firmly to the ground, providing a stable foundation. This meditation can be enhanced by visualizing the earth's energy flowing up through these roots, filling you with a sense of calm and stability. This practice is particularly useful after performing spells or rituals, as it helps to center your energy, ensuring you don't carry residual energies from your magical workings into your everyday life.

Methods for Regular Spiritual Cleansing

Regular spiritual cleansing is a crucial aspect of maintaining a healthy energy environment, both for yourself and your space. This practice helps in removing any lingering negativity, clearing away unwanted energies, and rejuvenating your aura.

One traditional method of spiritual cleansing is smudging with Sage or Palo Santo. Both these sacred herbs have been used for centuries in various cultures for their purifying properties. The process involves lighting the herb and allowing the smoke to envelop the area or person being cleansed. As the smoke rises, it attaches itself to negative energy, cleansing and clearing the space. When smudging, it's important to set a clear intention for what you're releasing, and to ensure proper ventilation for the smoke to leave, symbolizing the departure of negative energies.

Salt baths offer another effective way of spiritual cleansing, particularly beneficial after engaging in intense magical work or when feeling energetically overwhelmed. Sea salt, known for its purification properties, can help cleanse not just the physical body but also the energetic body or aura. Dissolving a handful of sea salt in a warm bath and soaking in it allows the salt's cleansing properties to wash over you, absorbing and neutralizing any negative energy clinging to your aura. This ritual can be enhanced by adding herbs or essential oils, aligning with your specific cleansing needs.

Sound cleansing, using instruments like bells, chimes, or singing bowls, is another powerful method to clear spaces and auras. The vibrations produced by these instruments are believed to break up stagnant or negative energy, restoring harmony and balance to the environment. The resonating sound waves emanating from these tools create a serene atmosphere and can be particularly effective in spaces where burning herbs isn't possible.

Regularly practicing spiritual shielding, grounding, and cleansing is essential for maintaining your well-being on your witchcraft journey. These practices form the foundation of your spiritual hygiene routine, ensuring that you remain protected, balanced, and clear from any energies that may hinder your practice. Remember, the key to effective spiritual safety lies in regular practice and intentionality, allowing you to deepen your craft in a protected and harmonious environment.

THE WICCAN REDE AND LAW OF THREEFOLD RETURN

In the practice of witchcraft, particularly within Wiccan traditions, ethical guidelines play a crucial role in guiding practitioners' actions and intentions. Two fundamental concepts that embody this ethical framework are the Wiccan Rede and the Law of Threefold Return.

The Wiccan Rede: A Guiding Principle

The Wiccan Rede, summarized in the phrase "An it harm none, do what ye will," serves as a core tenet in guiding moral decisions and actions within the craft. This principle encourages practitioners to pursue their will and desires as long as their actions do not cause harm to others, including themselves. It's a call for mindful living, respect for all beings, and taking responsibility for one's actions. The Rede's simplicity offers a broad and flexible guideline, allowing individuals to interpret and apply it based on their personal beliefs and circumstances. It emphasizes the importance of personal freedom and responsibility, urging practitioners to consider the consequences of their actions in all aspects of life, not just in magical practices.

Understanding the Law of Threefold Return

The Law of Threefold Return is another significant concept that complements the Wiccan Rede. It states that whatever energy a person puts out into the world, whether positive or negative, will be returned to them three times over. This belief encourages practitioners to consider the long-term effects of their actions and spells. The law serves as a reminder that all actions have repercussions, and these repercussions are magnified in their return. It's often interpreted as a kind of moral cause-and-effect, where kindness and positive actions lead to beneficial outcomes, while harm and negativity bring adverse consequences.

This law doesn't just apply to large or significant actions; it encompasses all aspects of life and practice. It teaches practitioners to be mindful of their thoughts, intentions, and energies, understanding that everything they release into the world will come back to them in a greater magnitude. It's about cultivating a practice and a way of life that's rooted in positivity, empathy, and conscious decision-making.

ETHICAL SPELLCASTING AND RESPECT FOR FREE WILL

The ethical implications of spellcasting are of paramount importance. Practitioners must navigate the delicate balance between wielding their power and respecting the autonomy and free will of others. This aspect of the craft is not just a matter of morality but also of the effectiveness and harmony of one's magical practice.

Understanding the Ethical Implications of Spellcasting

Spellcasting, at its core, is an exercise in directing energy to manifest a desired outcome. While this can be empowering, it also carries a significant responsibility. Ethical spellcasting involves being mindful of the intentions behind your spells and the potential impact they may have. It's crucial to consider not just what you are trying to achieve, but how it affects the world and people around you. This means avoiding spells that manipulate or harm others, infringe upon their free will, or produce unintended negative consequences. The ethical witch understands that every spell cast is a reflection of their own energy and intent, and by focusing on positive and constructive outcomes, they contribute to their personal growth and the greater good.

Respecting Free Will in Others

Central to ethical witchcraft is the respect for the free will of others. This principle dictates that imposing your will on someone else through magical means, without their explicit consent, is unethical. This includes a wide range of practices, from love spells aimed at a specific person to spells that seek to control or influence someone's decisions or actions. Respecting free will means acknowledging each individual's right to make their own choices and to experience their own life journey, without interference from external magical forces. Instead, ethical spellcasting focuses on spells that improve one's self, create positive environments, or provide support and healing to others who have asked for it.

NAVIGATING GREY AREAS AND EMBRACING ETHICAL PRACTICES IN WITCHCRAFT

Witchcraft, a path woven with mysticism and personal empowerment, inherently navigates through various shades of ethical complexities. The craft is not merely black and white; it thrives in grey areas, where the nuances of intention, impact, and moral judgment come into play. As practitioners, understanding and consciously navigating these grey areas is crucial for a practice that is not only powerful but also ethically sound and responsible.

The essence of ethical witchcraft lies in acknowledging and grappling with these complexities. For instance, the intention behind a spell might be pure, but the means and the impact require careful consideration. A spell cast to influence someone's feelings or decisions, even with the best intentions, raises questions about consent and ethical boundaries. Similarly, actions that might seem justifiable in the pursuit of a greater good can lead to unintended consequences, reminding practitioners of the delicate balance between personal will and the natural order. These scenarios call for a deep introspective understanding, urging witches to evaluate not just the immediate effects of their actions but also the broader ethical implications.

In addition to personal ethics, responsible witchcraft also involves being mindful of the sources and materials used in spells and rituals. Ethical sourcing of herbs, stones, and other ritual components is crucial, respecting not only the physical elements but also the cultural and spiritual traditions from which they may come. This mindfulness extends to environmental awareness, recognizing the impact of one's practice on the natural world and striving to minimize harm.

This journey of ethical witchcraft is not a set path but a dynamic process of learning, evolving, and adapting. It requires an ongoing commitment to self-reflection, a willingness to question and challenge one's own practices, and an openness to learn from the diverse perspectives within the witchcraft community. By embracing these principles, the practice of witchcraft transcends beyond personal empowerment to become a harmonious interaction with the larger tapestry of life.

Thus, navigating the grey areas and embracing ethical practices in witchcraft is about crafting a path that is in tune with the rhythms of nature, the principles of harmlessness, and a deep respect for the interconnectedness of all beings. It is about recognizing that each spell cast, each ritual performed, and each intention set is a thread in the larger weave of existence, holding the power to shape not just personal reality but the collective experience. This is the heart of a mindful and responsible witchcraft practice – a harmonious blend of power, wisdom, and ethical consciousness.

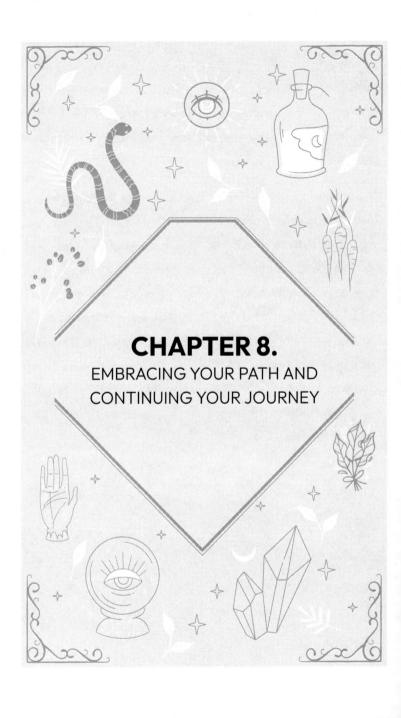

CHAPTER 8.

EMBRACING YOUR PATH AND
CONTINUING YOUR JOURNEY

As we approach the end of this enchanting journey through "101 Powerful Spells for Baby Witches," it's a moment ripe for reflection. You, the reader, have embarked on an extraordinary path, one that has led you through the intricate and mystical world of witchcraft. Each spell, each chapter, has been a step not only in learning the craft but also in personal growth and self-discovery.

From the first spell to the hundred-and-first, your journey has been about more than just acquiring knowledge; it has been about transformation. You've explored various facets of witchcraft - from casting your first spell to understanding the ethics and responsibilities that come with such power. Along the way, you've uncovered not just the secrets hidden in herbs, stones, and incantations, but also the hidden strengths and talents within yourself.

The practice of witchcraft is as much about personal empowerment as it is about magical prowess. Through this journey, you have learned to tap into your inner power, to harness the energies of the world around you, and to weave magic that is uniquely your own. This book has aimed to be more than a guide; it has sought to be a companion as you've taken your first steps into a larger, more magical world.

This path you've chosen is one rich with history, wisdom, and endless possibilities. The spells and practices you've learned are just the beginning. As you continue to grow and evolve in your craft, remember that each step forward is a testament to your courage, curiosity, and the vibrant spirit that defines a true witch.

In embracing witchcraft, you've not only embarked on a journey of learning but also on a journey of becoming. Becoming more attuned to the natural world, more connected to your inner self, and more aware of the vast tapestry of energy that weaves through all things. This journey is one of continual transformation, where each day brings new challenges, new joys, and new magic.

So as you reflect on the spells learned, the knowledge gained, and the personal growth experienced, know that this is just the beginning of a lifelong adventure. An adventure filled with mystery, power, and the endless potential of your own magical abilities.

CONSOLIDATING KNOWLEDGE AND SKILLS

As you turn the pages of this book it's important to pause and consolidate the wealth of knowledge and skills you've acquired through "101 Powerful Spells for Baby Witches." This journey has equipped you with more than just spells; it has laid the foundation for a deep and meaningful practice in witchcraft.

Essential Spellcasting Techniques

You've learned the art of crafting and casting spells, a skill at the heart of witchcraft. This includes understanding the significance of each component in a spell, from the herbs and colors used to the timing and phases of the moon. You've explored various methods of spellcasting, from simple candle magic to more complex rituals, each designed to harness specific energies and achieve diverse intentions.

Safety Practices in Witchcraft

An emphasis on safety, both physical and spiritual, has been a constant theme. You've learned how to responsibly handle candles, herbs, and other tools of the craft. More importantly, you've understood the necessity of grounding and centering yourself before and after spellwork, ensuring your energy remains balanced and protected.

Ethical Considerations

Ethics in witchcraft has been another key area of focus. You've delved into the importance of respecting free will, the consequences of your magical work, and the power of intention. The exploration of the Wiccan Rede and the Law of Threefold Return has highlighted the responsibility that comes with wielding magical power.

Development of Personal Intuition and Power

Perhaps most crucially, this journey has been about awakening and developing your personal intuition and power. You've learned to trust your instincts, to listen to the subtle whispers of your inner voice, and to tap into the unique magical abilities that lie within you.

As you continue to grow in your craft, remember that this book is a resource you can return to time and again. The chapters and spells contained within these pages will offer new insights and guidance as your practice deepens. Each revisit will reveal layers and nuances you may not have noticed before, reflecting your continuous growth as a practitioner of the craft.

Continuing Growth and Learning

Witchcraft is a dynamic and evolving practice, and this book is just the beginning of a lifelong journey. As you continue to grow in your craft, it's important to remain open to learning and expanding your knowledge. Revisit the chapters and spells in this book, as they will offer new insights and deeper understanding as your practice evolves.

Seek out additional resources to broaden your perspective and deepen your knowledge. This could be in the form of books, online courses, workshops, or joining local or online witchcraft communities. Engaging with other practitioners can provide valuable support, inspiration, and an exchange of ideas.

Remember, the path of witchcraft is as much about personal evolution as it is about magical practice. It's a journey of self-discovery, where each step forward opens new doors of understanding about the world around you and, more importantly, about yourself. Your growth as a witch will mirror your growth as a person – filled with learning, experiences, challenges, and achievements.

CLOSING RITUAL: A RITE OF PASSAGE AND BLESSING

As you stand at the threshold of a new chapter in your witchcraft journey, this closing ritual is designed to mark the end of your initial learning phase and to bless your path ahead. It is a ritual of gratitude, empowerment, and a blessing for your continued exploration and growth in the craft.

Preparing for the Ritual

- **Setting Up Your Space**: Choose a quiet and comfortable space where you can perform this ritual undisturbed. You might want to set up your altar with items that have become significant to you during your journey, such as candles, crystals, or symbols.

- **Gathering Essential Items**: You will need a white candle for purity and new beginnings, a small cup of water for cleansing, a piece of paper, and a pen.

The Ritual Steps

1. **Grounding and Centering**: Begin by grounding yourself. Take deep breaths, feeling your connection to the earth beneath you, centering your energy.

2. **Lighting the Candle**: Light the white candle, focusing on its flame. Let it symbolize the light of knowledge you've gained and the inner fire of your magical potential.

3. **Writing Down Your Gratitude and Intentions**: On the piece of paper, write down what you are grateful for from this learning phase. It could be new insights, personal growth, or specific spells that resonated with you. On the other side of the paper, write down your intentions and hopes for your future in witchcraft.

4. **Water Cleansing**: Dip your fingers in the cup of water and sprinkle a few drops over the paper. As the water touches the paper, visualize it cleansing and energizing your written words.

5. **Reciting Your Gratitude and Intentions**: Read aloud what you've written. Start with your gratitude, acknowledging and thanking the experiences and knowledge you've gained. Then, speak your intentions for your future practice, affirming your commitment to your continued growth in witchcraft.

6. **Closing Blessing**: After reading, hold the paper close to your heart and say, "With gratitude, I honor my journey thus far. With hope, I step forward into my continued path. Blessed be." Feel the energy of your words sealing your commitment.

Concluding the Ritual

- **Extinguishing the Candle**: Gently blow out the candle, symbolizing the end of one phase and the beginning of another.

- **Disposing of the Paper**: You may choose to keep the paper on your altar, bury it in the earth, or safely burn it, releasing your intentions to the universe.

- **Reflecting**: Spend a few moments in quiet reflection or meditation, feeling the energy of the ritual settle around you.

FINAL WORDS OF WISDOM AND ENCOURAGEMENT

A new chapter is upon you in your journey of witchcraft, remember that the path you walk is uniquely your own. Each spell you cast, each ritual you perform, is a reflection of your inner world, your hopes, dreams, and your profound connection with the universe. Embrace this path with confidence and a heart full of curiosity, for it is a journey that is as boundless as your own potential.

The craft you practice is more than just a series of spells or rituals; it's a dance with the energies of life, a harmonious blend of your will with the natural rhythms of the world. You are a weaver of magic, a creator of change, and a seeker of the deep, hidden truths of existence. Your practice is a powerful tool, not only for personal transformation but also for bringing about positive change in the world around you. With every spell you cast, you're sending ripples into the universe, ripples that can grow into waves of healing, love, and transformation.

As you continue on this enchanted path, let your heart be your guide. Trust in the wisdom that resides within you, the quiet voice of your intuition that whispers in moments of stillness. It will be your most loyal companion, guiding you towards your truth and illuminating your way through the shadows.

Remember, there will be moments of challenge just as there will be moments of triumph. Embrace them both with equal gratitude, for they are the teachers that will mold you into the witch—and the person—you are meant to be. Never forget that within you lies an incredible power, a spark of the divine, capable of shaping realities and touching the stars.

So, dear witch, as you close this chapter and step into the next phase of your magical journey, do so with an open heart and an unshakable belief in your own power. The world is waiting for your magic, your light, and your unique contribution to the tapestry of existence. Go forth and shine brightly, for in your journey of discovery and growth, you light the way for others to follow.

Blessed be on your path, for it is one of wonder, transformation, and profound beauty. May your journey be as limitless as the night sky and as deep as the deepest oceans. Remember, in the world of witchcraft, the only true limit is the breadth of your own imagination.

RESOURCES

As you continue to grow and evolve in your witchcraft practice, exploring additional resources can be immensely valuable. Here is a curated list of resources, including books, websites, and communities, to further enrich your journey in the craft:

Books

1. **"Wicca: A Guide for the Solitary Practitioner" by Scott Cunningham** - A comprehensive guide for individuals practicing on their own.

2. **"The Spiral Dance" by Starhawk** - A classic book that offers a deep dive into the rebirth of the Goddess religion and modern witchcraft.

3. **"The Green Witch" by Arin Murphy-Hiscock** - Focuses on the use of natural materials and elements in your practice.

4. **"Buckland's Complete Book of Witchcraft" by Raymond Buckland** - An in-depth exploration covering various aspects of Wiccan practice and theory.

5. **"The Inner Temple of Witchcraft: Magick, Meditation and Psychic Development" by Christopher Penczak** - A guide to developing psychic abilities and deepening your magical practice.

Websites and Online Platforms

1. **The Lost Book Project** - Of course, The Lost Book Project, a website dedication to the preservation, distribution and publication of rare, out-of-print esoteric texts and books.

2. **The Witches' Voice (witchvox.com)** - A comprehensive online resource with articles, local event listings, and a directory of witches and witchcraft practitioners.

3. **Llewellyn Worldwide (llewellyn.com)** - Offers a wide range of books and resources on witchcraft and metaphysical topics.

Communities and Forums

1. **Witchcraft and Wicca Facebook Groups** - Many Facebook groups offer a platform for witches to connect, share experiences, and seek guidance.

2. **Reddit Witchcraft Communities (e.g., r/witchcraft)** - Reddit has active communities where practitioners discuss various aspects of witchcraft and share resources.

3. **Meetup (meetup.com)** - Local Meetup groups for witches and Wiccans can be found in many areas,

offering a chance to connect with a community in person.

Podcasts and YouTube Channels

1. **"The Witch Wave" Podcast** - Hosted by Pam Grossman, this podcast delves into various topics related to witchcraft and magic.

2. **Harmony Nice** - A YouTube channel featuring a young witch sharing her experiences and knowledge about Wicca and witchcraft.

Online Courses and Workshops

1. **Witchcraft Foundation Course - Online Udemy Course** - Gain a solid Foundation for your Witchcraft practice.

2. **How To Write Your Own Spells - Online Udemy Course** - Published by The Lost Book Project by the brilliant Geraldine Egan.

These resources are just a starting point in your continued exploration of witchcraft. Each offers a unique perspective and depth of knowledge, helping to broaden your understanding and deepen your practice. Remember, the path of witchcraft is rich and varied, and there is always something new to learn and discover.

ABOUT THIS AUTHOR

Hazel Evermore, a name that has become synonymous with the contemporary witchcraft movement, hails from the mystical landscapes of the United Kingdom. With over two decades of dedicated practice, Hazel stands as a pillar in the witchcraft community, her journey reflecting a deep and abiding connection to the ancient craft.

Born and raised amidst the rolling hills and historical ruins that dot the British countryside, Hazel's affinity for witchcraft was evident from a young age. Her surroundings, rich in folklore and legend, provided the perfect backdrop for her to explore and hone her craft. Today, she continues to reside in the UK, drawing inspiration from its rich cultural heritage and the natural beauty that surrounds her.

Hazel's personal background is as diverse as it is fascinating. Over the years, she has delved deeply into various aspects of witchcraft, from traditional Wiccan practices to eclectic modern interpretations. Her approach to the craft is deeply personal and reflective of her journey, blending elements of nature worship, herbalism, and a strong belief in the power of personal intuition.

As an author, Hazel Evermore is passionate about themes that resonate with both the heart and spirit. Her writing often explores the intersection of the mundane and the magical, the power of the natural world, and the profound journey of self-discovery that witchcraft facilitates. She writes with a conviction that is born from experience, aiming to demystify the craft and make it accessible to all who seek its wisdom.

In her 20 years as a practicing witch, Hazel has not only deepened her personal practice but has also contributed significantly to the wider community. She holds qualifications in herbalism and natural magic, and her expertise is frequently sought in workshops and seminars. Though she is modest about her accomplishments, Hazel has been featured in several notable publications related to spirituality and witchcraft. Her work has also been recognized in various circles, earning her awards and accolades for her contributions to the craft.

Hazel Evermore's journey is a testament to the enduring power and relevance of witchcraft in the modern world. Through her writing, she continues to inspire, educate, and guide those who find themselves drawn to the ancient and ever-evolving path of the witch.

Made in United States
North Haven, CT
15 August 2024

56094397R00243